# THE BADASS GUIDE TO SUPERSTAR SELLING

*Delve Deeper, Sell Better, Achieve Faster Results*

Jackie Rainforth

Author: Jackie Rainforth
Title: THE BADASS GUIDE TO SUPERSTAR SELLING
ISBN: 978-1-77371-269-7
CATEGORY: BUSINESS & ECONOMICS/Sales & Selling/General
Publisher: Black Card Books
Division of Gerry Robert Enterprises Inc.
Suite 214, 5-18 Ringwood Drive
Stouffville, Ontario, Canada, L4A 0N2
International Calling: +1 877 280 8536
www.blackcardbooks.com



Printed in Canada

## TABLE OF CONTENTS

**ACKNOWLEDGEMENTS**

**INTRODUCTION – MY WHY** .......... 1

Enter the Rainmaker

What is a Badass Superstar?

Anyone Can Be a Badass Superstar

**CHAPTER 1**
**THE MODERN BADASS** .......... 12

Why the Need for Change?
World Events
    Be Genuine, Authentic, and Real
    Build the Bond of Trust
    Use Specifics
Old Perceptions and Stereotypes
    Serve Your Customer
    Saying Versus Doing
The Negative Purchase Experience
    Simplify the Process
    Everything Easy
Bigger Better Shinier
    Think Like a Customer
Tick Tock
    Be Ready for the Unexpected
Resources Are Tight
    Budget Before Anything
    Touch It – Feel It
Technology Today
    Strengths and Weaknesses
    Build Credibility and Authority
Competition Explosion
    Think Outside of the Box
Decision-Making Drawn Out
    Strategy and Patience

Social Media Stress
    Knock it Out of the Park
Customer Expectations on the Rise
    Personalization
    CRM
    Fast Isn't Fast Enough
    Partnerships in Performance

**CHAPTER 2**
**THE GENERATION GAP** ........ 39

Took It for Granted Boomers
The Game Changing Millennials
    Millennials are Cautious
    Millennials are Socially Conscious
    Millennials Put Family First
    Millennials are Price Sensitive
    Millennials Do Not Care About Brand
    Millennials Love Technology
    Millennials Love Shopping Online
    Millennials Love to Share Experience

**CHAPTER 3**
**MASTER THE BADASS MINDSET** ........ 47

Paralyzed by Fear?
Fear and the Next Step
The Stall Wall
Mental Blocks Disguised
Overcome the Mental Obstacles
Fearless? Think Again

**CHAPTER 4**
**GROW YOUR CIRCLE OF CONNECTIONS** ........ 58

Perfect the Power Intro
Nail Your Networking
Business Cards Still Matter
Meet and Greet Intros
Give the Best Gift Ever
    Law of Reciprocity

**CHAPTER 5**
**PROSPECT TO PROFIT** ........ 67

Propel Your Prospecting
Know Your Avatar
A Really Big List
The Gatekeeper
The Old-Fashioned Telephone Call
    Practice What You Will Say
    The Best Time to Call
    Leaving a Message
    Meaningful Voice Mail
    Busy or Ghosted?
Digital Prospecting and CRM
    Direct Email
    Opt-In Email Wave
Social Media Butterfly
Create a Personal Brand

**CHAPTER 6**
**DIFFERENTIATE TO ELEVATE** ........ 89

Product Differentiation
Knowledge Differentiation
Price Differentiation
Process Differentiation
Niche Differentiation
Exclusivity Differentiation
Service Differentiation

**CHAPTER 7**
**PREPARE, PREPARE, PREPARE** ........ 104

Be Enthusiastic and Energetic
Park the Ego
No Goals, No Growth
Continual Learning
Financial Analysis
Vehicle Kit
The Conversation Blueprint

**CHAPTER 8**
**BADASS SELLING - THE PRESENTATION** ............ 114

Build Real Rapport
Take Notes
Insightful and Provocative Questions
    Common Discovery Mistakes
    Questions to Delve in and Discover
Listen, Listen, Listen
Avoid the Product Dump

**CHAPTER 9**
**MEET NEEDS TO SUCCEED** ............ 124

Solution Resolution
The Real Reason
Deeper Emotional Need
    My Two Secret Words
    Know the Needs

**CHAPTER 10**
**WRAPPING IT UP** ............ 128

Test the Temperature
Easily Overcome Objections
Confident Closing
Now or Never

**CHAPTER 11**
**FIERCE FOLLOW UP** ............ 133

Process Is Proven
    Write to Ignite Follow Up
    Quote and Dote
The Lost Art of Thank You

**CHAPTER 12**
**THE NOTEABLES** ........ 138

Do Not Talk Price
Tell Stories and Give Examples
The Four Languages of Selling
    Presentation Extraordinaire
Make Them VIPs
Stand Out and Surprise
Action Paralysis
Upsell to Excel
    Do You Want Fries with That?
    Disservice Not to Offer Another Service
    Bundles Provide Benefits
Create Next Appointment
Ask for Referral
Poor Presentations Linger Long After
The Not-so-Fun Side of Selling
The Cookie Jar

**CHAPTER 13**
**FINAL THOUGHTS** ........ 152

**ABOUT THE AUTHOR** ........ 155

**REFERENCES** ........ 156

# ACKNOWLEDGEMENTS

To my husband Doug, my rock, thank you for always believing in me, for filling my life with fun, and for your encouragement to follow my passion in making this dream come true. But most of all, for loving me without fail.

To my beloved children, all my favorites, Brittney, Austin and Joel. The love, laughter and happiness that you bring to my life reminds me of how blessed I am every day.

To my brother Greg, who has been my mentor, sounding board and best friend for all these years. Words cannot express how much you mean to me.

And to my team (Marcy, Jill and Jennifer) and girlfriend Barb, thank you for the guidance and support you have provided on this incredible journey.

To all the mentors (George Dramalis, Ron Bryant, Uri Hess, Pat Adams and Malcolm Sissons) and those special people who have made such a profound difference in my career and to those who have contributed to the book, thank you.

To all the incredible customers who have supported me over the years, it would not have been possible without you!

A heartfelt thank you to all!

# INTRODUCTION – MY WHY

Sometimes, your life needs to be disrupted—shaken out of routine, so you can scale new heights. This is my story.

Always one to take on excitement and high risk, scuba diving was another item on my bucket list. I took the lessons, did a few small dives, and on a glorious sunny day, my husband and I headed out to have the time of our lives. Off the island of Cozumel, Mexico, in full gear, I jumped off the back of the boat and down I went. A little slow at first, my weights a little heavy, I sank 40 feet below the surface.

It was spectacular! Holding hands with my hubby, Doug, we were looking around, laughing, enjoying all the Caribbean Sea and Mother Nature had to offer.

One of the guys we were diving with motioned to take my photo. With two big thumbs up, I was living life to the fullest, or so I thought…

After the photo was taken the fellow diver and Doug turned and swam forward. I turned to follow. Then it happened.

I wasn't getting any air. I couldn't breathe!

In my mind I'm thinking, "I must have swallowed water." Mentally berating myself for being so stupid, I longingly looked off in the distance for Doug. He does not see that I am in trouble. "Uh-oh, I'm on my own."

Thinking back to the lessons, I quickly blow out my regulator.

Nothing.

I could feel my lungs slowly filling up cm by cm. It was the most eerie feeling. I blew out the regulator again. Nothing.

Uh-oh. I was in trouble. Serious trouble.

Panic? No, not really. Fear? Yes, kind of… but a weird, calm fear.

I felt myself slipping… slipping away...

I blacked out into darkness…

Then, I saw the most magnificent bright light! And I felt the most overwhelming love for Doug and the kids! It was like a big warm blanket that enveloped me! It was glorious! If I could keep this moment forever.

Weird, Doug is now standing face to face, only a foot away. I can almost touch him?! What?

I am feeling really confused! He was so far away? And now he is right in front of me??

He is sad. So sad. I can feel his sadness as he is slowly waving and whispering a gentle melancholy 'good-bye'?! My heart feels searing pain rip through my body! Noooooo! I don't understand?! What is going on??

I was tearlessly crying. Soundlessly screaming. A deep sorrow uncontrollably engulfs me.

Then, with a snap of a finger…

It dawns on me where I was and what was happening.

I look up and beggingly say "NO! PLEASE!!!... I don't want to go…"

Then I hear a voice say, "Jackie, you have missed all the signs. You have been blessed with many gifts and talents—share your experience with others to help them feel more confident and successful. Make the lives of others better, easier… You have an amazing new path ahead of you."

I abruptly come to.

The Dive Master is aggressively shaking me and tapping his fingers on my face mask and pointing at his. He is desperately trying to get my attention and get me to focus on him. (He later he told me he saw my body go limp and my eyes roll to the back of my head.)

I was groggy and weak, like you feel when coming out of surgery. My eyes stayed locked on his; as I longingly clung to him as my lifeline—my survival. He shared his regulator. Air yes – but I wasn't getting much?!

I was physically exhausted, barely able to lift a limb. I clung to him with all my might as he clipped my body to his and pointed to the surface. He slowly brought me up to the top. He inflated my vest as I lay on the surface, bobbing at the whim of the waves. I greedily gasp for air, coughing and spitting up blood and phlegm. He waved the boat over. They helped me on board and peeled off the heavy equipment.

Onboard, I was coughing like crazy. A deep nasty cough that I couldn't stop.

Water. I drank water as I tried to calm my cough. The men were still diving.

Jose, my Dive Master was saying they needed to get me to the hospital. I could see the worry on his face but brushed it off. "No, no, I'm fine," I say. "Let's go back in!" I was trying to hide my embarrassment and shame. No way was he letting me back in the water. He repeated himself, "We need to get you to the hospital."

About 20 minutes later, the guys came up from their dive. One look at me and Doug immediately knew something was wrong. I felt safe and secure at the sight of him. The tears welled up in my eyes.

He sat down beside me as Jose explained the stark reality of what he witnessed. My husband was horrified. He had no idea what had happened down below. He looked at me lovingly, with extreme worry and concern. I try to reassure them both, "No, I'm fine. I'll be okay."

The boat was a good distance off shore. As we headed back, not only was the cough getting worse, now I was making a funny wheezing noise. It was getting hard to breathe again.

Without warning, I was hit with the most searing pain in my right temple. It felt like someone was hammering a stake into the side of my head. It was like no pain I had ever felt before. It was horrific. Okay, I get it. I agreed to go to the hospital.

As soon as the boat got back to shore, the Dive Master Jose, hailed a cab and immediately got us to the hospital. The doctor on call did a quick assessment, then stated, "I need a second opinion." And they rushed me into the emergency room, where as quickly clothes were being peeled off, lines were being stuck in and oxygen was flowing through a mask. Ah! Finally, I could breathe without pain! Poor Doug. He looked so worried. An ultrasound of my lungs was showing black and white fuzzy lines like an old tv when the cable went dead, "not good," they said.

I was admitted to ICU. My body had swollen up like a balloon. Massive needles and three types of oxygen pumped through me. I was still so weak and exhausted.

The Director of the hospital came daily to check on me. He said I had a rare and unexplained condition called IPE Immersion Pulmonary Edema, where my body couldn't tolerate negative water pressure. The capillaries in my lungs had collapsed and filled with fluid, a condition they called internal drowning. My heart had stopped, which is why I blacked out and crossed over.

It turns out the searing pain was due to a lack of oxygen to my brain. My blood pressure, which was normally low, had skyrocketed. He continued with, "More than fifty per cent of people with this condition die in the water. Of the 50% that make it out, 35% die before they get to a hospital." Yes, I am truly blessed!

I spent three days in critical condition, in a state of grogginess, yet my head was spinning, reliving the experience, trying to grasp the enormity of it all. What did that message mean? What was I supposed to do? I was feeling so thankful and blessed. The others were concerned, yet I was just thankful to be alive. In my mind, it was a true miracle. My beloved husband faithfully stayed by my side, day and night. Jose stayed the full three days to help translate before I was stable enough to leave. On day four, I left the hospital, deciding like all girls would, to take the opportunity to go to the gift store just down the street towards the taxi stand.

It was here that I experienced yet another episode where I felt myself start to pass out. I couldn't breathe – but I caught myself. Was this real? My imagination? By now, I was experiencing overwhelming fear? I was beyond terrified! Telling myself to remain calm, I focused and savored each long, deep and forced breath. We quickly went back to the hotel so I could rest. But I wasn't allowed to go home. We were told to spend five more days in Mexico. They were concerned about the high-pressure effects of flying.

When we arrived home in Canada, I was on strict bed rest for six weeks. Worried that I had serious heart and lung damage, my doctor put me through a barrage of testing. Miraculously, no long-term effects. Each day I relived the incident, as the message consumed my thoughts. I looked back over my life and now knew what I had to do. My greatest joy throughout my career had been training others and seeing them excel.

I later found out that there are over 100 dive shops on the island of Cozumel with less than 20% of them having access to the private scuba hospital I was taken to. The doctors at this specific hospital were all internists, highly trained abroad in scuba and scuba injury, and all were advanced divers themselves. Because of this, they were able to diagnose my very rare condition. Had I been taken to a regular hospital, I likely would have died.

I call Jose Maria Losano, the Dive Master, and now my beloved friend, my angel on earth. Not only did he save my life in the water that day, but he saved my life a second time when he insisted that we go to the hospital. I will always be eternally grateful!

Upon reflection, the reality of what had happened and the many blessings I had been given began to sink in; a very precious gift… one that I am thankful for each and every day. One I did not want to waste.

My career as a sales trainer and this book, are the path I needed to follow from the message I received that day, back in May 2016.

I hope the information contained in this book inspires you to expand your reach and set your sights on even greater achievements. Listen to your intuition, notice the patterns that are around you and remember to live each day to the fullest. Everyone has a personal definition of success. Let the contents of this book be the catalyst to achieving yours.

## ENTER THE RAINMAKER

**A BADASS is thankful and appreciative of blessings and opportunities.**

The message went around and around in my head for days, *"Jackie you have been blessed with many gifts and talents—share your experience with others to help them feel more confident and successful. You have an amazing new path ahead of you."*

I instinctively knew that training is what I was meant to do. For years, my greatest joy had been training salespeople and watching them rise to incredible levels of success. Now it was all making sense.

In the beginning of my career, I was a complete disaster. But here is the cool thing… I quickly went from a selling disaster to becoming the top sales performer at every company I ever worked for; breaking records, winning awards, and receiving accolades. I helped to change industries along the way.

My career in the residential construction world did leaps and bounds. I have been blessed to work with some of the most incredible people, companies and customers who have given me the greatest of opportunities.

In the corporate world, I went from a B2B sales rep to Regional Sales Manager, finally landing as Director of Sales and Marketing for the second largest plumbing company in Canada.

As an entrepreneur, I owned my own sales agency representing the global brand, American Standard. My success there won me the coveted nomination of *RBC Women Entrepreneur of Canada Award.*

I have an unparalleled understanding of the sales industry as my roles have given me a 360-degree perspective from all perspectives; the seller, the buyer, the prospect, the decision maker, the leader, the executive and as a sales trainer. Selling is my passion.

The success I achieved earned me the name "THE RAINMAKER" by my peers.

> **Rainmaker:** ***1. One who is known for the exceptional ability to attract new clients, generate business and bring intangible prestige to an organization based on his associations and contacts. 2. A person who makes it rain cash.***

But like I said, it did not start out that way.

The development of my proven program came from my own personal growth journey from disaster to BADASS. I take a unique but simple approach to selling.

By applying my formula of strategies, tips, techniques and approaches, I have actively trained a vast number of salespeople to achieve phenomenal sales success. Many are now owners of their own companies, manage organizations or they continue to hold the top sales leader designations within their respective industries. They are BADASS SUPERSTARS.

## WHAT IS A BADASS SUPERSTAR?

> **BADASS** ***adj: 1. A general term used to describe behavior that is fearless, authentic, compassionate and ethical. 2. Well above the standard for normal behavior. 3. Exceptional and excellent. 4. Stays true to themselves, not being fake to impress others. 5. Does not give up, pushing themselves for the better, no matter how hard it gets.***

A BADASS consistently knocks it out of the park. They have incomparable closing ratios, a funnel regularly filled with new customers, a loyal and dedicated base of repeat and referral clientele and extraordinary incomes. They have a simple, yet reliable skill set that makes building rapport, overcoming objections and closing easy. They have acquired the simple and easy techniques that allow them to delve deeper, sell better and achieve faster results, while catapulting their sales.

A BADASS SUPERSTAR continually asks themselves these questions:

1. **What can I do to serve my customer better?**
2. **How can improve my customer experience or outcome?**
3. **How can I differentiate?**
4. **What 'value-add' can I provide?**

Selling is the most incredible profession. Whether you are a seasoned veteran, new to sales, leading a sales team, or an owner of your own business, we all have the desire to increase our sales and improve our performance so that we can earn a higher income. What other job affords us such an incredible opportunity?

The problem is, it can be extremely stressful and all-consuming because our income is directly related to how good we are at our craft. It can be an emotional rollercoaster, with the highs being a big celebration and a sense of incredible accomplishment, through to the lows where we feel like a failure, beat ourselves up, live with never-ending guilt, wondering how and where it went so wrong.

The dejection and frustration we as salespeople can feel day after day hearing the word 'no', having doors slammed in our faces or conversations cut short with the ominous silence of phone line gone dead, can take its toll. Or what about consistently calling on the same customers, but never seeing any results? Or worse yet, never getting a response from a prospect after repeated attempts? For some salespeople and owners, the mental consequences escalate to overwhelming, as they endlessly worry about losing their jobs, their businesses and the ability to support themselves and their families.

Regardless of our circumstances, where we are on the pendulum, or what type of position we hold, if we are selling a product or a service, we are all chasing the elusive and forever moving carrot that dangles in front of us. We all continue to search for the secret words or magical methodology that will help us become better so we can improve our closing ratios, catapult our sales, and earn the incomes and lifestyles we yearn for. We hope that we can one day achieve BADASS SUPERSTAR status. We want to be fierce, confident and outstanding.

Some people start off with a natural talent, but for most of us, it is a journey. Getting there is about taking one step at a time, making minor, incremental changes, 10% at a time to master the task or concept, and then moving onto the next level, simultaneously improving confidence levels.

## ANYONE CAN BE A BADASS SUPERSTAR

**A BADASS knows performance is an attitude.**

Think about a horse race. All the horses start off the same, yet only one horse crosses the finish line before the others, resulting in earnings ten times more than the other horses. Is he ten times better? No. He usually does not win by much, often just a nose, only a few seconds faster. In selling, it is the same thing. You don't have to be ten times better, instead, make small adjustments that will give you the advantage. The culmination of multiple small changes, over time, will help you achieve substantive and progressive success.

***"Superstars do the things that others won't,***
***so they can live life like others don't."***

—Jackie Rainforth

If I can do it, and the people I have trained can do it, you can too.

We all have the desire to increase our sales and improve our performance so that we can earn a higher income. What other job affords us such an incredible opportunity?

***"Success is nothing more than a few simple disciplines practiced every day."***

—Jim Rohn

A BADASS SUPERSTAR is the standard of excellence that is required in this new era of selling. It is about stepping forward and presenting yourself as prepared, knowledgeable and consistent in all that you do with the ability to shift, flex and pivot. Questions and responses need to be delivered seamlessly, with impact and confidence. BADASS SUPERSTARS have a simple yet reliable skillset that make building rapport, overcoming objections and closing easy. Techniques that allow them to delve deeper, sell better and achieve faster results, and catapult their sales results.

# CHAPTER 1

# *The Modern* BADASS

**A BADASS makes the selling experience better because they are people-focused.**

I have salespeople approaching me saying. "I'm not getting the results I used to. It is so much harder. It's never been like this before! What is going on?"

A new modern approach to sales training has emerged due to societal changes. Economic models have been replaced with a focus on emotion based or psychological models of selling. The old scripted way of selling doesn't work. When we try to implement the script with today's customer, instead of coming across as professional, we are perceived as phony and self-serving. It alienates the customer and results in missed sales and reduced income generating opportunities.

The BADASS needs to be proficient in confidence, knowledge, communication and skill. Having the 'gift of gab' is not enough.

## WHY THE NEED FOR CHANGE?

### The BADASS understands that SELLING HAS CHANGED!

Maximizing our opportunities is the key to becoming a BADASS SUPERSTAR. Today, we are faced with obstacles that have made the art of selling much more difficult than ever before. We need to take a different approach. Recognizing those changes and shifting the way we sell, takes us one step closer to becoming a BADASS SUPERSTAR.

## WORLD EVENTS

**A BADASS never loses their optimism.**

Events over the last two decades have dramatically changed the world we live in. We have seen a cultural shift in buyers to one of deep seeded skepticism, distrust and resistance. The sales process, how we buy and how we sell has been forever changed based on the following events:

- **The Unfathomable Terrorist Attacks of 9/11:** 2,996 people killed, 6000 injured, and caused at least $10 billion in infrastructure and property damage. Plus, the multitude of attacks that have happened since and continue to occur; **society is more fearful and cautious than ever before.**
- **Economic Catastrophes Such as the USA Housing Crisis:** 10 million families were tossed from their homes onto the streets and the financial institutions that were believed to be fail-safe, simply crumbled; **there is an increased need for economic self-preservation to reduce personal risk.**
- **European Debt Crisis:** Portugal, Italy, Greece and Spain (The PIGS Nations) required national financial bailouts resulting in bleak economic futures and severe austerity programs for their citizens; unprecedented unemployment rates, lowered wages, increased taxes and loss of social programs. They will continue to feel the consequences of these events for generations; **an underlying anxiety is brewing regarding a potential global domino effect, loss of faith in governments, and the inability to control.**

- **Random Rampage Shootings and Massacres:** The senseless and heartbreaking loss of innocent people and children. The only thing we can ask is why? **People are more cautious and suspicious, with heightened levels of fear.**
- **Ethics Violations and Corporate Fraud:** Large organizations such as the Enron, Lehman Bros., Bernard L. Madoff Investment Securities and Sears Canada where company leaders bilked employees and investors out of their life savings and pensions, leaving them penniless. Boundless greed by a few that ruined the lives of so many; **the sense of trust is obliterated and faith in guarantees is questioned. People now assume hidden intentions and motivations.**

Twenty-five years ago, we couldn't have imagined these horrific, life-altering events happening. The consequences of the above events have monumentally altered how we as a society think. It has resulted in significant shifts in our natural instincts of trust, hope and optimism, to one of uncertainty, skepticism and distrust.

***"Only 1/3 of Americans trust other people – the lowest level recorded since the General Social Survey first began tracking trust levels since 1972."***

—Forbes

The mistrust and resistance prevalent in today's society has magnified the obstacles in selling. The need to find a better way to sell has never before been so important.

## Be Genuine, Authentic, and Real

Gone are the days when salespeople had automatic credibility and authority. Today, because of the distrust and resistance that exists, we need to earn the right. The BADASS knows they have to know you, like you and trust you before they will buy from you. One must sell themselves before they can sell their product. And of course, actions speak louder than words.

This is the biggest concept or movement in modern selling. Being transparent and forthright allows us to connect and build solid, meaningful relationships with one another. The more natural and honest you are at having conversations with people, the more successful you will be and the deeper the connection you will have with your client.

As Tony Suberlak, my lawyer, friend and Partner at Masuch Law LLP says,

***"How you present yourself is very important. Just be yourself! Don't try to put up false fronts to play a role or impress someone. Don't be afraid to be vulnerable, to open up or share your personal life. People will tend to trust you more."***

Others can tell when you are being genuine versus faking it and they will respond better to you being you, versus the non-intimacy of wearing your "salesman only" hat. The more they like you and trust you, the increased likelihood that they will become a loyal repeat customer, which is what we all want as salespeople. Today, selling better is about building deeper relationships with an honest and transparent exchange of information.

## Build the Bond of Trust

Trust has never been so important. When people distrust, chemicals are released in their brains causing anxiety which quickly turns to stress. We subconsciously fear those we do not trust. Fear that they are going to be ripped off, taken advantage of or duped.

Since 85% of the sale is based on the relationship and only 15% is product knowledge (Brian Tracy), a foundation where the relationship is based on trust is of utmost importance. People are naturally resistant to the selling process and will put their guard up. When they purchase, they are looking for someone who won't steer them wrong. Investing time and effort to bridge that gap is a crucial step in selling. True influence is derived by consistently providing value combined with honesty and integrity.

### Use Specifics

Providing specifics about your process, methodologies, system and how the numbers were derived, helps the customer feel more secure in the purchasing process. Giving them an understanding of what they can expect or a mapped process that lets them know what is coming and what the results will be in the end, provides assurance.

If you cannot build a bond of trust, you will not get the sale. It all starts with you, then the company and finally your product. Trust on all levels is essential in becoming a BADASS SUPERSTAR.

## OLD PERCEPTIONS AND STEREOTYPES

**The BADASS works hard to conduct his business with character, not just charisma.**

One of the biggest problems salespeople still struggle with today, are the negative perceptions and stereotypes that have transcended over time. Selling started with the door to door salesman peddling goods and services that homesteaders needed to survive. The products sold were critical and necessary.

The onset of the Industrial Revolution after the world wars, saw an explosion in manufacturing. An influx of new inventions promised an easier lifestyle and demand for these products made selling a simple easy process.

In the 1950s and 1960s, selling started to change. Instead of the simple presentations that were product-centric, salesmen started selling with PIZZAZZ. Personality, charisma and the ability to "wow" people became more important than the product. As a result, people's needs took a backseat to the sale; the goal, flash over substance.

The stereotype of a sleazy, cigar smoking, used car guy emerged. Slick gimmicky lines and activities manipulated people into buying. Cash took precedence over caring. The only goal these salesmen had was to sell the product and earn the commission. Customer needs were not on the salesperson's radar. When the products didn't stand up to what people were told when sold, consumers felt deceived.

Selling then moved into a more sophisticated and structured "scripted" scenario. The internet and the customer's ability to do research did not exist, meaning the salesman controlled the information and the process, making the selling cycle, predictable and manipulatable. The salesman had control. He followed a script using pre-determined lines to hook the customer making them an easy prey. The customer often did not find out the valuable information he needed that would have altered his buying decision, until it was too late. He felt duped.

Fast forward to today and unfortunately, the old stereotype of the aggressive and greedy salesman still exists. Have you ever been through a high-pressure timeshare experience or had a salesperson trail closely behind you in a store? And we can't forget about the guy who insistently pushes you to get the extended warranty. How does this make us feel? We avoid the salesperson and the sales process whenever possible.

Regrettably, bad selling practices where people feel bullied, continue to thrive, perpetuating the old, negative image. It causes many buyers to be highly suspicious, doubting the honesty and motives of salespeople.

## Serve Your Customer

The BADASS focuses on his customer, not the sale. Serving the customer and being buyer-centric, are the most dominant ideologies behind modern selling. They are the difference between the old scripted methodologies of the past and "the know you–like you–trust you" concepts of today. However, finding a balance between serving your customers and making decisions that are self-serving can be difficult, especially for those on 100% commission. If salespeople come across as self-focused and too aggressive. They end up alienating the customer.

**TIP: High-pressure salespeople who focus on their needs might get the order the first time, but they will not get the repeat sale. In selling today, customer needs must always come first.**

## Saying Versus Doing

**A BADASS knows that integrity is the cornerstone of all success.**

Selling today is about being honest, truthful and accurate. It is about consistently living by a set of strong moral principles and about following through on the commitments you make. As a salesperson and as organizations, we must be uncompromising in our adherence to the principles of honor, fairness, and decency.

Every day, we are presented with moments where our integrity can be compromised. How many times do we say we will get together for coffee, or give someone a call, knowing full well we never will? Or have you ever told someone the delivery is en route when you know it wasn't? We can justify it by saying it is just a small fib, but every time we do or say something that is not quite true, we eat away at our integrity. Wouldn't it be a lot easier and less complicated if we were honest at all times? Something to think about.

Words easily lose their meaning. Actions create impact and impact is what people remember and respect.

When I first started selling, I had a customer, a Purchasing Manager, who always accepted my appointment requests. He explained that it drove him crazy when representatives would show up late. He said he had 50 reps a day calling on him, yet regularly, many would arrive late. He said he used it to cull the crowd. He chose to accept meeting requests and purchase only from those who were punctual and respectful of his time.

**TIP: Statistics list being late as one of the biggest frustrations, customers have with salespeople. If you commit to a time, show up 15 minutes early.**

It seems like a small thing, but often there is a lot more at stake. Greg Butt, Director of Canada for White Rogers, my brother, advisor and mentor reminds us:

***"Do what you say, say what you mean. Integrity is doing the right thing, even when your customers and managers aren't looking."***

Omitting and misrepresenting the truth are the same as lying. Hoping things miraculously resolve themselves before your customers find out is naive. Customers always find out. They may not say anything, but you will see and feel the consequences. One little 'mistruth' can severely jeopardize the relationship and any future opportunities. Marlene Cameron, my coach from Marlene Cameron Coaching sums it up well:

***"Being in alignment and in integrity radiates authenticity and presence."***

# THE NEGATIVE PURCHASE EXPERIENCE

**The BADASS knows an obstacle is an opportunity in disguise.**

Too often, customers have made purchases only to be left feeling swindled, exploited or run through the wringer. Their unpleasant experience left them feeling resentful and angry. As a result, they become defensive, expecting the worst, with a "me against them" attitude. They believe they know what is coming and what to expect when in a sales situation and prefer to walk away or use the automatic response of "no, not interested." What the customer fears most is:

- Paying too much for a product, finding they could get a better price elsewhere.
- Being wronged, in terms of being ripped off.
- Buying the wrong product being stuck with it.
- Having the product break down, with no recourse.

We all have had those negative purchasing experiences where what should be a pleasant experience, it becomes one of anger and frustration. As a result, purchasers feel forced to raise their wall, be on guard and protect themselves from letting it happen again. It is easier to avoid than potentially being at risk.

## Simplify the Process

We all understand that it is important to be upfront and honest about our business and our product lines. But what many may find uncomfortable, is that in today's selling environment, with the introduction and advancement of the Internet, it is becoming increasingly vital to show the price.

I once worked for a company who gave an "all in" parts and labour price. When customers asked for a breakdown, they were denied. It enraged people because they couldn't see what they were paying for.

This type of pricing policy will have little tolerance as we move forward into the future. Customers will simply stop buying.

Today, companies are being much more candid in discussing their pricing, focusing instead on the value-add benefits they provide. Modern sellers know that this type of candid approach builds the foundation for long term, loyal relationships.

## Everything Easy

**A BADASS knows that there is much more to selling, than simply closing the sale.**

Selling has moved to a buyer-centric focus, with the customer centre stage. In order to drive profitability and gain a competitive advantage, BADASS SUPERSTARS know that it is crucial that customers have a positive experience, both at the original point of sale and after the sale is complete.

Organizations and salespeople alike need to have a system in place if the product or service is deemed unsatisfactory.

As the Sales Agency representing a large manufacturer, customers were frustrated that they had to phone a 1-800 number to get parts. Yes, the company had a system in place, but it was not as convenient or timely as it could be. Clients had to wait on the phone for far too long and they felt like they had to jump hoops to get after-products.

In order to solve, I worked with a couple of local suppliers to implement a parts program. It was a win/win for all. The contractors could pick up the parts at their convenience, instead of having to wait days to receive. Their clients were happy because their service needs were addressed immediately. The suppliers gained an additional source of high margin revenue that took up very little space, and we as the agent, no longer received calls from unhappy contractors. A win/win for all.

With the overwhelming competition that exists today, companies and their representatives need to examine every aspect of their process. Even the smallest kink in the wheel of customer service experience could easily prompt a customer to move their business elsewhere.

## BIGGER BETTER SHINIER

**The BADASS knows they need to be on target, if they want to win with today's customer.**

Today, salespeople are often trying to convince customers to buy something they already have, only bigger, better, newer, fancier. They may not see any worthiness in replacing what they already have. This makes the selling process a lot more difficult and competitive.

For salespeople to move them off the ledge of indecision, they must create value that the customer perceives as important. Customers must also visually see themselves using the product or service, and they must know what the end-experience will be, in terms of how they will benefit.

### Think Like a Customer

A big mistake I see salespeople make, is that they focus on features and benefits that they think are important, yet they forget to focus on what the client sees as important.

Everyone is different. When people go to purchase a car, they often buy for different reasons. Some might want speed and status, while others might want comfort and seating configuration.

If you want to sell something bigger, better and shinier, every action you take in selling must be from the customer's perspective.

To present points that support the comfort and roominess of a car, when the buyer is looking for speed and status will not get you the sale. This is a highly exaggerated example, but I see salespeople go through features and benefits that have zero relevance, all the time. It is like throwing mud on a wall, hoping something sticks. And worse yet, it diminishes their professionalism and credibility with the client because they appear to not have paid attention to the clients needs.

Instead, find out what the customer requirements are by asking quality questions and then become highly targeted in your focus. If you present only those things that the customer sees as valuable, supporting every selling point with their end desire, you will motivate the customer to move forward in the selling process and achieve faster sales results.

## TICK TOCK

**The BADASS SUPERSTAR respects time as money.**

As companies are downsizing and merging, leaders and owners are asking employees to do more with less. Time has become an extremely valuable commodity. Prospects do not have a lot of time to allocate to salespeople. Leisurely conversations where a sales rep could sit down and have a relaxed and lengthy presentation, asking multiple "discovery" questions, are no longer acceptable. Those days are long gone. Now, people are annoyed by those who waste their valuable time asking questions they should already know the answers to. The salesperson today needs to do thorough research and be fully prepared with a basic understanding of the customer, the company, and the challenges they face. They must be prepared to bring solutions, before they meet with the customer—solutions that resolve the issues that exist for the customer.

Asking discovery questions during the presentation is only to confirm you are on track. They are a benefit to the seller, not the buyer, therefore they must be kept to a minimum. Statistics show during your first meeting with a C-Suite prospect, the average of only four discovery questions is allowed before each additional question thereafter reduces your odds of closing the deal and starts to become counterproductive.

C-Suite Executives and business owners want salespeople to alert them to threats and opportunities they have not seen. They want to be educated with information, trends and industry news. True value comes from those representatives who can make their clients aware of how their current situation is no longer viable and how it can be improved. Be a loss aversion specialist, not a time aversion specialist. Today's BADASS SUPERSTARS will have done thorough research and have a strategic plan with clear objectives to assists the customer, in place for every call.

## Be Ready for the Unexpected

**A BADASS prepares for the unexpected and is ready for anything that comes.**

Before you can call on someone to promote your business, one must have the knowledge and the tools in place, to strategically prepare for success. It is surprising to see how many people in sales do not take the time to prepare, and simply "wing it". In fact, 50% have no idea what questions they are going to ask when they walk into a meeting. You only get one opportunity to make a great first impression.

## RESOURCES ARE TIGHT

**The BADASS SUPERSTARS are respectful of budget.**

Another societal change affecting how we sell today, is that households and organizations simply do not have the resources they used to. Getting people to part with those resources is becoming more difficult. Gone are the materialistic days of the 1980s where overspending and excess were the norms. Fear of economic uncertainty and instability have created a value in society where reducing debt load, being financially conservative and saving is now the new standard to be pursued. BADASS SUPERSTARS need to be value sellers.

Statistics show cost of living and net incomes are slowly eroding. All this means your dollar continues to buy less than it did the year before. How we sell, engage and captivate customer attention, and encourage them to part with their buying dollar, will become progressively more difficult. The motivators making customers more inclined to part with their limited resources will be:

- Creating a return on investment.
- Increasing revenue and profitability.
- Saving time or money.
- Improving efficiency.
- Loss and risk avoidance.

### Budget Before Anything

Today, depending on the product or service, ask about the budget up front. "Do you have a certain budget in mind?" It will give you an opportunity to identify the best product or service solution. The bonus, they could have a much higher budget than anticipated, giving you the opportunity to start high.

## Touch It – Feel It

Product sampling ranks as one of the most effective methods of marketing. Excitement and appeal is created by effectively showing the client what the real working experience and benefit for them will be. People and companies have fewer resources, and they are still anxious about the current economy, making them discriminatory about their purchases and the products they use. This makes sampling more important today than ever before. It is a trial experience that allows customers to interact with the product, giving them the kinesthetic experience to determine whether they are going to like it, while visualizing how it will work for *them.*

***"More than half of prospects want to see how the product works on the first call."***

—Hubspot

An added benefit of sampling is that it takes the pressure off the salesperson because the focus can be on the product.

**TIP: Always leave a takeaway with the client and have extras as they may request multiples for additional decision makers or team review. It is a strategic reminder for the prospect to follow up, confirm a decision, or share with others, including internal members, or for other network referrals.**

# TECHNOLOGY TODAY

### The BADASS knows everyone is watching.

Every day there is something new, better or faster. The explosion of technology has led to more knowledgeable, informed and empowered customers. Clients today often know more about you, your product and your competition, than ever before. In the past, salespeople would present the products, price points, and specifications. This is often no longer required as customers do their own research online, discovering the potential solutions, social proof, testimonials and word-of-mouth experiences. They closely watch how negative reviews are handled by the organization. They may or may not purchase online, but they do make a buying decision based on all the information they have gathered. And then, only then may they reach out to a sales representative.

***"As much as 60%–70% of the customer's decision-making process is done without ever having to engage with a salesperson."***

—Brevet

***"Ninety per cent of consumers read online reviews before visiting a business."***

—Forbes

The standard sales presentation has shifted from one of information provider, where the salesperson had control over the process and the facts to more of an advisory consultative position. The role of the salesperson is now meant to support the customer through their sales journey, but the majority of their input, is in their final stages of the purchasing process. The days of having orderly and predictable selling stages that are easy to follow are not as clear or foreseeable as they used to be.

## Strengths and Weaknesses

Carefully designed questions are required in selling today to deliver the most feedback and information possible. It is important for the salesperson to discover how much research the prospect or customer has done, and what degree of knowledge they have with regards to you, your competitor and pricing. Being a knowledgeable expert in your industry has been more important.

Knowledge is power. Knowing the strengths and weaknesses that you, your company and your product bring to the table and the benefits they provide is essential in selling. How are you better, unique or different than others in your industry who are vying for the same business? Know how to turn your weaknesses into strengths and how to overcome all objections.

## Build Credibility and Authority

Word of mouth and social proof are essential in earning trust, particularly for the Millennials. Use positive reviews and testimonials to your advantage. Bring them with you on a sales call, place them on your website, post them on social media. They should be paired with a photo and placed at the top of your landing page, on display in your showroom or visitor locations and sales representatives should also use and verbally promote when face-to-face with clients.

It will make people feel more confident in doing business with you.

**TIP: Show human faces and team photos on your websites and social media pages help people identify with your team. People feel more confident and secure knowing there is a team behind you.**

## COMPETITION EXPLOSION

**The BADASS doesn't let competition scare him, he uses it to motivate him.**

Competition is everywhere! In the past we would worry about a few local competitors. Now with the click of a mouse, your customers have access to a multitude of hungry global competitors. Because many are web-based versus brick and mortar, they do not typically carry the same overhead. Having lower costs drastically changes the financial criteria of the sale process.

Margins and inventory turnover are imperative to profitability. They can make or break a company's cash flow and financial success. Knowing your numbers not only from a selling perspective but also in terms of the company point of view is now a must-do for today's sales professionals.

With resources being tighter than ever before and the significant increase in competition, companies and sales representatives need to understand that they will need to be delve deeper, sell better and achieve faster results if they want to successful. Creating impact, differentiation and providing value-added benefits to serve customers more precisely and effectively, will be the standard moving forward.

### Think Outside of the Box

When I first started selling American Standard, I was up against well-established competitors. I felt blocked everywhere I turned.

The Hutterites, however, were a group that were virtually non-serviced in our industry. I saw the gap and an opportunity to thrive. They had incredible potential.

As a group, we soon understood that the Hutterites valued quality over anything else. As each colony hit 100 families, they would buy more land and build a new colony requiring homes, barns, plumbing and electrical buildings etc., all requiring new bathrooms and bathroom fixtures. Their product of choice was a top of the line, high margin fixture that was reliable, dependable and came with a ten-year warranty.

We, as a sales agency, were the first to consistently call on and serve this incredibly loyal and powerful buying group. We provided a high caliber product with solid pricing and second to none customer service. Word of mouth spread like wildfire, which resulted in us having the most incredibly loyal and dedicated group of customers and unique niche market. They still have a very special place in my heart, as we built many lasting relationships.

**TIP: Always look at ways to be unique and different. Think outside the box, outside the norm, beyond the status quo.**

## DECISION-MAKING DRAWN OUT

**The BADASS SUPERSTAR is strategic and patient but works to achieve faster results.**

Many organizations have shifted from vertical integration and individual decision making to a matrix models and collaborative processes. In the past, having one decision maker was the norm. Currently, there are often multiple people involved in closing the deal. Group decisions systematically ensure everyone's needs are met, while also generating new ideas and catching or exposing unintentional errors.

***"In a typical firm with 100-500 employees, an average of seven people are involved in most buying decisions."***

—Brevet

This has exponentially complicated the sales process as individuals have different needs and priorities, extending the time and resources required. Buy-in will be stretched, and unfortunately, there a greater likelihood of losing the sale will exist.

### Strategy and Patience

The BADASS knows the decision-making process will take longer, and will ask up front, "When it comes to making decisions like this, do you consult anyone else? Are there others that should be involved?" If yes, scheduling a meeting with all the key participants would be the ideal next step in efforts to foster a more successful outcome.

## SOCIAL MEDIA STRESS

**The BADASS knows word of mouth is the best type of advertising.**

The impact of social media cannot be overlooked. The BADASS knows social media has changed the rules. With distrust being a societal characteristic, word-of-mouth referrals, social proof and customer testimonials are now the most powerful marketing factors to drive trust and potential sales.

***"Ninety-two per cent of consumers believe recommendations from friends and family over all forms of advertising."***

—Neilson

***"Ninety-four per cent say an online review has convinced them to avoid a business."***

—Review Trackers

When the consumer advocates for a product, service or company, trust is automatically transferred. Social media is an extension of that. How you conduct your day-to-day business is now reported on a transactional, minute by minute basis. A disgruntled or happily satisfied customer can report his or her experience within minutes, resulting in an immediate impact on your sales, your reputation and your bottom line. How you respond to the feedback received can make or break a person's decision to buy from you.

A large kitchen appliance manufacturer was having a flood of angry reviews and comments online. Instead of being transparent and upfront, the company simply responded with "Please contact our customer service department." This was a colossal fail in today's era of selling. New customers want to see how the company is prepared to handle complaints, as it provides an expectation of the customer service level new customers can expect. The appliance company had the opportunity to use the social media platform to their advantage, by showing 'yes, we have an issue, but rest-assured we will do everything in our power to fix it'. But instead, the non-transparent path they chose, likely compromised their brand's credibility and trust, losing potential customers forever. Customers understand problems will arise, but when they do, it is how they are handled that matters most.

Acknowledge the comment within 24 hours. Be positive and exhibit a serving attitude. Make the efforts to resolve the issue quickly and professionally. Going the extra mile for an unhappy customer will serve you well. Good, bad or ugly, social media is out there for all the world to see and it is a very powerful influence.

***"It is 5 to 25 times more expensive to acquire a new customer than it is to keep them."***

—HelpScout

## Knock It Out of the Park

**As BADASS SUPERSTARS, we look to create impact in our customer experiences.**

With social proof being so significant, the impact of testimonials cannot be understated. Today more than ever, they need to be used to build credibility, authority, and trust. One of my favorite testimonial examples, probably because she was a small business and I wasn't expecting it:

I was looking to hire a dog sitter to stay in my home and watch my pups. I had not used Pawz Pads Plus services before, nor was I familiar with using this type of business in the past. I will be honest, I had reservations, leaving my beloved dogs overnight in my home with a stranger.

She blew away all my expectations and fears when she opened her binder. First, she showed me her "Animal CPR Certification", I didn't even know there was a accreditation for animal CPR. Then page by page she went through an array of testimonials from previous clients, ending with a copy of a report card she would fill out upon completion of her dog sitting. WOW! I was impressed. Did she earn my trust? You bet.

She was professional and took her business seriously. Social proof reduced my scepticism, resistance and fears, helping me to make the decision to hire her.

***"Sixty-eight per cent of people will pay more for a product or service if value is proven."***

—Forbes

With social proof becoming such a determining factor in the decision-making process, salespeople should regularly pursue personal and company testimonials, letters of reference, awards and certifications.

Every salesperson and business owner should have a brag book filled with their personal and company testimonials. They should take it on introductory calls and show it to their potential clients. Not only will it build trust, it shows your professionalism on a completely different level, helping you stand out amongst the competition, making an impact with prospective new customers.

## CUSTOMER EXPECTATIONS ON THE RISE

**The BADASS knows that excelling in customer service is the priority in modern selling.**

We live in the Age of Excellence—a time when customer expectations have hit an all-time high.

As a BADASS SUPERSTAR we must exceed expectations, not simply meet them. Today, we must be partners with their clients. The expectancy in the past was to have a quality service at a fair price. Now, it is much higher. Today salespeople and companies must be proactive, delivering a personalized, connected, immediate and seamless experience. Customers expect a WOW customer experience at every touch point.

The importance of providing outstanding customer service goes without saying. Customers want to know that as their partner and ally in the business, you will resolve any issues. They understand problems will arise, but when they do, it is how you handle them that matters. For example, they want a risk-free experience. If a product fails to meet expectations, in any way, they want the reassurances to be able to return the goods in a 30-day period, no questions asked.

They also expect to receive an immediate response when they make an inquiry, regardless of whether that is via phone, email or a social media platform.

***"82% of consumers expect immediate response on sales or marketing questions."***

—Small Business Trends

If you as a salesperson cannot personally resolve the situation and must pass them on to someone else within your organization, customers expect a "connected" experience. Their information, past interactions, and history need to be known and understood, making the transition and their overall experience seamless. Having CRM or Customer Relations Management Software is ideal for this application, as notes are written in the system by an individual are available for all staff to see, quickly providing the customer situational awareness that is expected by purchasers in our modern era.

## Personalization

Today's consumer wants to be able to pick and choose various options or select between product offerings, allowing them to personalize their purchase. This means delving deeper to learn more about them as individuals, their wants and preferences but also understanding their specific challenges. Companies then take that data and make customized suggestions that add value, efficiency, simplicity or improvement.

My father-in-law deals with a retail menswear store. They keep track of his sizing and style, color and brand preferences. Over the years they have gotten to know him very well. Whenever a product comes in that they know suits his taste, the salesman picks up the phone and calls to let him know. They will put together ensembles, based on his personal style and have them ready and waiting for him to come view.

As time passes, this type of scenario will become increasingly more common as companies try to increase their loyal, repeat customer base through improved customer satisfaction levels.

Smart companies and salespeople who want to build their businesses and keep customers coming back, will increasingly focus on providing this type of personalized service. My father-in-law shops nowhere else, and when he goes in, you can be assured he spends a lot more than the cost of the singular item they called him to see.

## CRM

**The BADASS knows technology is an essential part of modern selling.**

CRM is an acronym for Customer Relationship Management software. It helps you gather, track, store and manage customer data, keeping an accurate and accessible record of customer interactions. It assists in maximizing personalization, creates and monitors regular email campaigns with opt-ins that consistently grow the database, all of which has become a priceless sales resource in our digital world. CRM software assists you in all forms of readiness for customer interaction and can accommodate beginner to advanced. I have used Maximizer, CRM for years. It has greatly contributed to my sales success.

## Fast Isn't Fast Enough

Customers want instantaneous responses from their sales representatives and the companies they are choosing to deal with. When looking for answers they expect a call back right away, or at least a text telling them when they can expect to hear from someone. Technology has pushed us into a state of immediacy that can ultimately help us win or lose the sale.

> ***"Thirty to fifty per cent of sales go to the vendor that responds first. Immediacy is now the new rule."***
>
> —Brevet

## Partnerships in Performance

Customer involvement is a new service development process. As we become increasingly "buyer-centric" focused, the expectation by customers is that they have the ability to contribute and provide input. Companies and salespeople who take a more evolved customer approach; those who listen and respond to client feedback and encourage interaction, will rise to the top as we move forward.

Customers want to contribute input and they want to be heard. They want to let you know how your product or service can be improved and better meet their needs. Businesses who listen to customer feedback, identifying the specific wants and needs of their clients and incorporate those changes in their product offering, will be rewarded with increased loyalty and support. The introduction of new products and their ability to reach specific target markets will be vastly improved as a result.

Many years ago, I used to work for a company called I-XL Brick Supplies Ltd. as a Technical Sales Representative. Luxury home builders and designers wanted more contemporary colors.

At the time, red-coloured brick was the standard. By asking for their opinion and listening to their feedback I found out the specifics of what was missing in our product line. I understood exactly what they were looking for, because of their input. I was able to present suggestions to my superiors. At the time, the Company who had a relatively small percentage of this high-end market. New home buyers were choosing the more cost effective and versatile color palette of the stucco products. The President immediately and impressively responded to my suggestions. Remarkably, he personally sent me down to the manufacturing plant to work with the head engineer. We were able to create six new colors based on customer recommendations. The new product line exploded onto the market with phenomenal results. Not only did sales skyrocket, we were able to access a new luxury and design-based target market; one that we were virtually non-existent in before.

***"Research shows 76% of customers expect companies to understand their needs and expectations yet feel only 13% of customers believe a salesperson can understand their needs."***

—Brevet

Customers should be treated like people, not numbers. We must be open, honest and listen to their wants and need, treating feedback as a gift not a criticism. Competition abounds. If we cannot meet these new higher expectations, both as companies and as sales representatives, clients will not think twice about taking their purchasing dollar elsewhere. Just ask Kodak, Block Buster, Blackberry and the numerous other giants who failed to respond.

# CHAPTER 2

# *The* GENERATION GAP

**The BADASS respects old wisdom and looks forward to the new.**

The BADASS knows times and values have shifted dramatically. Not only have world events changed our customer, but for the first time in history, we are selling to multiple generations in the workplace. All have varying, often contradictory beliefs, politics and values. The two predominant groups in the workplace are the Boomers and the Millennials. It is important to understand what makes these groups different and how it affects selling.

## TOOK IT FOR GRANTED BOOMERS

**The BADASS respects experience and wisdom.**

Although the Baby Boomer generation is losing its foothold in the marketplace to the Millennials, there's still value in understanding their mindset. You never know when you'll be in a meeting caught between the two generations. Understanding how each of them thinks will help you to bridge the gap, should the need arise.

The Baby Boomer generation is the post-war babies born from 1946–1964, a population explosion as a result of the veterans returning from the war with new hopes and optimism for the future. Known for their affluence and large disposable incomes, they are big spenders, taking consumerism to the extreme, often criticized as in excess.

They have represented an era of prosperity and abundance that has eroded into a much different world for the more conservative and financially cautious Millennials. This has resulted in a more difficult selling process for those in the selling profession.

Boomers are traditionalists who value hard work, loyalty and follow through. Work-centric, they are highly competitive and goal oriented, often basing their self-worth and identity on their workplace achievements, performance and titles. They like formal communication, preferably face to face and as a group they are serious and focused, often prioritizing work over family. Hesitation is not a factor when it comes to after hour events or time away from home. They like the perks and prestige of the VIP experiences and giveaways.

Acknowledging their achievements, showing signs of respect and giving praise for their experience and expertise are the ways to win over this confident group. They are open minded and like to learn, valuing the educational aspect you bring forth as a salesperson. Boomers believe there is a formal and established way of doing things, so do not cut corners with them.

Following through on your commitments is the number one priority when calling on this generational group as they will use to it judge your level of professionalism and determine your worthiness as a representative. Be straight forward when talking or presenting to this experienced group, letting them take the lead will help you build rapport and strengthen your relationship with them.

## THE GAME-CHANGING MILLENNIALS

**The BADASS knows Millennials have changed how we sell and go to market.**

The laid back, idea sharing, collaborative Millennials share values that are vastly different from the formality of the "play-by-the-rules" Boomers. As we move forward in time, it is important to understand those differences and adapt our selling because the entrance of this generational group is changing how we as salespeople need to go to market. If you are a veteran salesperson, it is essential to familiarize yourself with these demographic variations. The basic skillsets of the past are less relevant as selling has evolved and will continue to advance into a much more multi-dimensional process.

Those born between 1981 and 1996, the Millennials, are currently ranked as the largest generational group in the workforce.

***"By 2025, 75% of the Workplace will be comprised of Millennials."***

—Harvard Business Review

Although the Boomers still hold 80% of the USA personal net worth and experience, the Millennials are fast becoming *the decision makers of today and the future.*

***"From 2015-2018, 87% of Millennials in the workforce took on management positions at their companies."***

—Neil Patel

This highly innovative and technological group is all about social consciousness, improved work-life balance, and a propensity for team-oriented, collaborative environments. They are politically active and have no problem speaking up for what they believe in. They expect relationships that thrive on open, honest and transparent interaction. This is far different from the "do as I say, do not question" beliefs of the hierarchical Boomers.

Liberal, and team oriented, the Millennials are on the opposite end of the pendulum to the work-centric, work-hard play-hard Boomers who value corporate climbing and competitiveness. The differences have created tension as each group has difficulties understanding the other, often resulting in judgement and criticism.

- **Millennials are Cautious:** Not only have the Millennials witnessed economic and world chaos, but they also entered the workforce with sky-high unemployment rates, reduced wages and an increasingly expensive cost of living. As a result, they are far, less optimistic and naive. They are extremely cautious and fearful of debt.

***"65% of Millennials do not use credit cards, preferring pre-paid cards or cash."***

—Bloomberg

They want truth and transparency. Building a relationship of trust is absolutely necessary with this group. If you treat them right, you will have much higher engagement and loyalty levels than that of their Boomer predecessors.

- **Millennials are Socially Conscious:** Millennials want to know that the companies they are supporting are making a meaningful difference and direct impact in their communities and the world. Social consciousness is prioritized precedence for this influential group.

***"Thirty-seven per cent of Millennials say they are willing to purchase a product or service that supports a cause they believe in, even if it means paying extra. Seventy-five per cent of Millennials want companies to give back to society with their profits."***

—Neil Patel

Making sure Millennials know that your firm supports charities is an important factor in reaching the Millennial decision maker as it could easily sway their choice of product or provider.

- **Millennials Put Family First:** After watching their workaholic baby boomer parents suffer from burnout, stress and health issues, the balance between home and family is a non-negotiable for the Millennials. They are a generation who places tremendous value on "living life to the fullest" and spending time with their children. Where the boomers revelled in after-hour events, Millennials would prefer to be at home with their families. Children, activities and partners are good topics of conversation for building rapport. Respecting their weekends and after-hours time will be vital.

- **Millennials are Price Sensitive:** The Millennials have seen reckless overspending, mismanagement, loss of millions of jobs to outsourcing, and poor financial decision made by governments all of which have led them to be more cautious, price sensitive and politically motivated. Millennials do not have an equal income to that of the Boomer at the same stage of life and they are saddled with higher schooling costs.

***"Forty-six per cent of Millennials hold school debt compared to only thirteen percent of the Boomers."***

—Yahoo Finance, Cameron Huddleston

The economy is much different today, versus the thriving economy of their parents' generation.

***"In 2017, it was found that Millennials made 20% less than boomers did at the same age."***

—Huffington Post / Michael Hobbes

Millennials have been thrown into a situation where their lack of resources, combined with weak labor markets, poor economic conditions and unusually tight credit conditions, have left them no alternative, forcing them to be more responsible and frugal, with less inclination to waste their hard-earned money.

- **Millennials Do Not Care About Brand:** Where the boomers were brand driven, the Millennial is not. When Baby Boomers experienced product failures, they would be left frustrated and bitter because they didn't have time to deal with issues. It created a significant move to more expensive brand-name products because the well-established companies had higher perceived value in the area of reliability. That is not the case today. Millennials can research the product online, using reviews and social proof to determine which products are reliable. Their only concerns are price and whether that price is in line with their perceived value and requirement to have on-time delivery.

- **Millennials Love Technology:** This new generation has been raised on high tech innovation and use it as a staple resource. They rely on their smartphones, computers and tablets using them automatically and immediately. They will research you, your company, your competitors, your product and pricing as well look at all online reviews and every social media platform. All this means that as the sales representative, having exemplary levels of product knowledge and market intelligence is essential. Salespeople need to be perceived as experts in the field to attract, retain and win over the Millennials.

- **Millennials Love Shopping Online:** Time is valued, so team this with technology and you have created the perfect solution… online shopping. Why would Millennials waste time browsing in a store when with a click of their fingertips they can buy anything they desire online and have it delivered right to their door? Brick and mortar companies are falling out of favour with this generation and becoming victims of organizations like Amazon.

> ***"Millennials are buying from Amazon at a higher rate than their older or younger generational counterparts, with 79% or 3 out of 4 Millennials making purchases online."***
>
> —Cision

Online shopping has changed the economic landscape and has become both a real and threatening issue for traditional retail. The ongoing closures of retail stores is a grim reminder of a trend that is accelerating and changing the shopping process. All the large department store chains like Walmart, Best Buy and Home Depot have adapted on-line shopping to their service offering. A costly manoeuvre, but they are fully aware of how they need to attract, entice and hold onto the younger, up and coming generation of shoppers.

- **Millennials Love to Share Experience:** They do not hesitate to share their purchasing experiences, good or bad, on all social media platforms because they as a group rely on and embrace social proof. They trust the experience and feedback of others exponentially more than traditional advertising or marketing.

***"Ninety-five per cent of Millennials say that friends are the most credible source of product information."***

—Neil Patel

If you want to drive sales with this powerful and influential audience, you will need to maximize your technological visibility, improve your accessibility, and ensure your personal and company brand is pristine. With "word of mouth" virtually the only factor to rank in building trust with this cohort; companies and their representatives have to concentrate on supporting and encouraging external public reviews, consistently providing social proof via testimonials and make sure that sharing with their friends is easy to do when they choose your brand.

You can guarantee this demographic shift has had an enormous effect on modern day selling. As salespeople, it is our responsibility to understand the generational differences and be able to quickly shift if we want to bridge the divide and attract this emergent and powerful group of Millennials.

# CHAPTER 3

# *Master the* BADASS MINDSET

**A BADASS knows that mind is a powerful influence that breaks down mental boundaries.**

Before you can efficiently and effectively share your product, service or talents, you must be confident enough to face your fears. I am the first to admit, it is not easy.

Mindset is the one thing that truly differentiates a BADASS from the pack. It is a priority if one wants to tackle the challenges we face today and rise above the rest as SUPERSTARS. A positive attitude, the yearning to learn, and the ability to delve deep through personal self-reflection and self-awareness are enviable and sought-after traits in today's professionals. But the one word that truly describes a BADASS SUPERSTAR, is FEARLESS.

Regardless of where we are in our career, facing fear is a constant hurdle. All of us, will at one time or another hit a plateau where our mindset is going to make the difference between keeping us stuck, or moving us forward.

Selling is the business of creating new business. Yet this is the one area where most people freeze. There are two types of fear; fear of failure and fear of rejection. We worry about doing or saying the wrong thing, looking foolish, or not meeting the expectations of others. Fear stops us from making cold calls, knocking on doors, and following up on leads.

## PARALYZED BY FEAR?

**The BADASS knows fear can stop you in your tracks and impair more than income.**

I started my career with great intention, excited at the possibilities and completely confident that I would succeed. But instead, I was a complete disaster.

I kind of fell into my selling career. I was at University and took a summer job as a receptionist. My boss at the time, George Dramalis, an incredibly wonderful man, saw something in me that I did not see in myself. He said I had 'personality' and promoted me to sales. I had all the right mindset qualities; the personality, attitude, yearning to learn and the desire to serve. But I was missing something instrumental: the ability to move past my fear.

I was selling time clocks to businesses that needed their staff to punch in and out, recording the times they started and stopped working. As a one-time, single transaction sale with very little chance of getting repeat business in the future, I needed to cold call to create business. The company put me on a "draw", meaning I would get a guaranteed base salary but needed to pay it back if I fell short in achieving my sales/commission goals for the month.

I started making cold calls, but I did so randomly without a plan. If a business had employees, I called on them. Each day I went out and consistently received "NO-NO-NO". And when I was able to land a meeting, I didn't know my product very well. We had a new computerized time clock. I knew the basic marketing features and benefits but had no idea how to use it. As a result, the meeting would end quickly, and I of course did not get the sale. I left feeling humiliated and defeated. I felt like a giant failure. Over time, I started doing less and less. It got so bad that I would check in at the office in the morning and again at the end of the day, only to show my face and pretend I was working. During the day I sat at home watching TV, all day, every day. It was awful. I felt like such a fraud.

Month after month my self-esteem cratered, and I sunk lower and lower. I desperately hoped for orders that were telephoned into the office as they generated the income I badly needed.

The entire façade began to affect every aspect of my life. It became intolerably exhausting. It did not take long before I had become a depressed and ashamed couch potato. I was completely stuck, paralyzed by inaction and rejection.

Afraid to be found out and totally disgraced, I quit and found another job.

## FEAR AND THE NEXT STEP

**The BADASS knows fear is a state of mind and that changing self-talk is the first step.**

At the new job, I knew I would need to change if I was going to make it in sales. I recognized that it was fear holding me back. I was still feeling like a fraud, but I made small incremental steps to overcome the mental blocks that were immobilizing me. I changed my self-talk to "I can do this!" and "I will be successful in sales!"

My boss at the time, Ron Bryant, a truly brilliant salesman, was the manager at AMES BROS TILE AND STONE. He took me to the next level. He guided, challenged and supported me every step of the way. His lessons were instrumental in setting me up for sales success. Ron taught me:

- **Look for Opportunities in Unique Places:** Find leads and opportunities in places most people neglect to look. I learned to be attentive and cognizant of the potential that existed, in out of the norm places like billboards, magazine ads, association listings, and construction signs.
- **Focus on a highly defined target market.** Focus on customers that I knew would be in the market for my product and do so with a targeted plan. Do not waste time calling on prospects that have not been substantiated or researched.
- **Take action.** Get out and do something, regardless of how small. Start off with baby steps and soon they will grow into giant leaps.

With these three valuable lessons in mind, my closing ratio started to increase. I was not a BADASS yet, but I was feeling more comfortable and self-assured. Each call took me one step closer towards building the success and the income I longed for. And the best part, I was no longer a couch surfer!

**TIP: Depending on your industry, leads can be found in newspapers, reports, magazines, construction signs, advertisements, social media, directories, newsletters, and community papers.**

## THE STALL WALL

**The BADASS knows that the key to success is action.**

No matter how hard we try, fear appears. It is that invisible line that abruptly stops us in our tracks, and all our efforts completely stall. I call it the STALL WALL. We don't see it, but we always, always feel it. They are the mental blocks that hold us back; fear, rejection, lack of confidence, lack of belongingness, and the old tapes from our childhood… "I'm not good enough! I'll never be successful! I don't belong!"

The STALL WALL stops us from taking the action we need to keep moving forward. The negative, subconscious, self-sabotaging things that we say and think to ourselves. The binds that hold us hostage and keep us from doing what we know we need to do.

***"Successful people control their inner dialogues. A successful person thinks successful thoughts."***

—Brian Tracy

Wendy Going, GM Calgary Division/Managing Partner of Timber-Tech Truss and one of the most inspirational leaders I have ever known says:

***"You need to push yourself out of the comfort zone in everything you do. If you sit back, you will never know what you are capable of. If it scares you—you're making the right choice."***

## MENTAL BLOCKS DISGUISED

**THE BADASS knows procrastination is the thief of opportunity.**

The mental blocks we carry will often show up disguised in the form of procrastination, and sometimes even perfectionism. You know you are stuck when you start doing the following avoidance activities:

- **Busyness:** You find an endless array of things to do. By keeping busy, you avoid the tasks you know you should be doing.
- **Make Excuses:** Excusing you from doing what you should be doing. "Oh, I need to get this done first", "This is a

priority right now", "I have to do this instead". Anything and everything will become the priority over doing the tasks you should be concentrating on.

- **Hanging at the Office:** You choose to hang out in the office, wasting time chatting or socializing with staff.
- **Sitting Around at Home:** I know, NONE OF US DO THIS… sitting at home on your couch watching TV instead of getting out there and making calls.
- **Extra Long Lunches or Golf:** You book never-ending lunches that last for hours instead of using the time to prospect and drum up new business. Or golf booked during the day instead of late afternoon.
- **Arrive Late/Leave Early:** If we shorten our day, we can convince ourselves that we have put in a good effort.
- **Comfortable Customers:** You hang out with the same old customers. The ones you like, that you know well, who are nice and safe and keep you in your comfort zone when you should be out prospecting and creating new customers.
- **Overwhelmed in Administration:** Routine tasks such answering emails takes precedence.
- **Job Hopping:** You constantly switch jobs because you know you are not out there hunting, and fear being found out. You tell yourself, "this isn't the job for me".

These are all choices. If you find yourself making any of these, seriously ask yourself if fear is holding you back?

***"The average salesperson only sells 1.5 hours per day, with the first call made at 11 a.m."***

—Brian Tracy

If fear and rejection were non-existent, do you not think people would be rushing out the door, selling ten hours a day, every day? Procrastination robs us of opportunities and success.

## OVERCOME THE MENTAL OBSTACLES

**The BADASS realizes the biggest obstacles are the barriers created in our own minds.**

It is the thought process we have that creates the fears we experience. It is all about mindset.

The good news, if fears are learned… they can be unlearned. Recognize fear and the discomfort it brings. Remind yourself, "Fear is only a state of mind. I am outside of my comfort zone." Visualize the stall wall and push through the fear knowing that you are in a position of growth and learning. This is how I did it:

- **Be Prepared:** Understand your product inside and out. Be the expert. Recognize your strengths and weaknesses and those of your competitors, plus take it one step further, know how to maximize your personal strengths and downplay your weaknesses. Then, create a process and a plan that is consistent and will provide added confidence that can be relied on in times of stress or unnerving.

- **Look at Your Time Management:** Be honest with yourself. What are your inefficiencies? Where could you improve? Are your mental blocks disguised as procrastination? Are you wasting your time with social media and other forms of distraction?

- **Eliminate the Excuses:** Stop pointing the finger and placing blame on others. "If my company did this" "If my boss did that" "If the market was better, if only…" Deal with what you have and make it happen with the tools and circumstances that you have today. Superstars are completely responsible for their actions and accountable for their results.

- **Do Not Take It Personally:** This is business… they aren't saying NO to you personally, they are saying NO to what you are offering. Hold your head high and be excited that you are taking action and achieving your goals.
- **Write Down "What is the Worst that Can Happen?":** The word NO only has the impact you place on it. You will wake up tomorrow with family and friends who love and adore you. Nothing can change that.
- **Keep Track and Make It a Game:** Rejection is part of sales. Understand your sales funnel numbers and make it a game instead of a point of personal rejection. If you know you need to make 1,000 phone calls to get 100 prospects, and 100 prospects lead to getting ten customers. Know your ratios and understand that you are going to get a lot of NO's. Use your time to practise improving your skillset. Keep track of the calls and the results. Remember, you have a 50/50 chance of receiving a YES response.

***"You miss 100% of the shots you don't take."***

—Wayne Gretzky

- **Reframe the Self-Talk:** Our thoughts fuel our feelings. Create a different inner dialogue and silence the negative thoughts.

***"We all have the power to choose***
***what kinds of thoughts take up space in our mind.***
***The fact that you sometimes produce negative thoughts***
***doesn't mean you have to accept them unconditionally."***

—Selling Power

# FEARLESS? THINK AGAIN

**A BADASS SUPERSTAR knows that fear is a persistent hurdle to overcome.**

A couple of decades after mastering the fear of cold calling, and ranking as a record-breaking, elite sales performer, I was once again challenged and surprised by my old buddy, fear. What I did not realize is that fear can hit us an any time in our career, regardless of how sophisticated our skillset has become. The process is the same, but this time, I realized you also must have faith in yourself, follow your gut, and understand that other people's opinions are none of your business.

Tony Testini, who grew to be a good friend, was Regional Manager at American Standard Canada. He believed in me and took a chance, giving me the opportunity of a lifetime. He and Harry Kandilas, a true business "fixer", the Business Leader for Canada, gave me the rights to represent and sell the giant and well-known global manufacturing brand American Standard, under my own Sales Agency. I was thrilled! It involved setting up my own company, hiring, training and leading employees, and running the sales and operations within the territory. I was up for the challenge! It was 100% commission based. I had no direct experience with the product or the distribution channel, but I had a successful selling system, strong work ethic and a belief in myself and my ability.

Once the company was established, I learned the products, and started creating my strategies and processes. The Western Regional Head Office of our largest supplier called me in for an initial visit. I walked in to see six executives, all dressed in suits, looking very professional. I was excited and somewhat intimidated meeting them. They asked me questions about my new business and my strategy to cover the enormous territory as a mere team of two. I thought things were going well, that they understood my vision and plan for execution. Sure, the sales representative I originally hired fell through and I didn't have another one in place, yet, but I would. And sure, they had a legion of branches that needed to be called on. "My soon-to-be hired employee and I could do it." I said. Originally, feeling quite confident, I was starting to shrink.

As the meeting came to an end they said, "We didn't want American Standard to hire you. We wanted a larger, experienced agent to represent the line."

OUCH! The words stung.

With my mind spinning, I was feeling totally deflated. Devastated actually, but I didn't let it show. As we were exiting towards the door, I summed up all my bravado and said, "Thank you for your candour. Please know that I will do my best; please see what I can do before you pass judgement."

Oh my. It felt like an out of body experience. I remember in that moment the fear rushed over me like a tidal wave. The old tapes that had lay dormant for so long had now been triggered and were screaming in my head. "How could I be so stupid?" "I was NEVER going to be able to do this!" I was horrified that I was going to fail, that I wasn't good enough, that I would make a gigantic fool of myself, especially in front of the two people, whom I wanted to make proud; who believed in me enough to hire me.

I recognized the feelings. I had to immediately push the fear aside and go full throttle through the STALL WALL that wanted to hold me back. I had to believe in myself, keep my inner critic quiet, trust my gut and repeat to myself, "I know I can do this!"

In four short years, I persevered and under my tenure, American Standard went from the bottom of industry ranking to the number one position in the province. Using the same successful techniques that I had developed over the years, I grew the company, expanding and training a team of "non-industry, non-experienced" people, into industry BADASS SUPERSTARS.

The results equated to a sales increase of 280% in four short years, totalling millions of dollars. As a result, I received the coveted nomination for the *RBC Women Entrepreneur of Canada Award.* I never expected to have my work recognized like that. And I especially couldn't have imagined it when I was starting out. Wow! It is amazing what you can achieve when you put your head down and just keep taking one step at a time.

I used those same, highly successful and proven techniques as the foundation for my current 5-Part SUPERSTAR Excellence Selling program that is based on incremental learning and client customization. It has substantially increased sales for my clients, many have seen increases over 20%.

The lesson here is to believe in yourself at all times. Yes, there will be times when you feel fear, but keep your eye on the target, trust your gut, and think back to the past successes you have achieved. Do not let people and their negative opinions sidetrack you. Positive thoughts only.

A quick trick I learned to do that was to recollect an extremely successful time or event in your life. The brain will release all the endorphins you felt in that past moment of success, allowing you to experience physiological benefits in the current moment, moving you from fear to confidence.

Face your fears head on with fortitude and courage and push through the wall knowing there will be success on the other side. You never know what astonishing outcome could be waiting.

# CHAPTER 4

# *Grow Your Circle of* CONNECTIONS

**BADASS SUPERSTARS maximize opportunities to meet others.**

Your first introduction must have impact. Whether it is in networking, a referral meetup or conducting a presentation, how you introduce yourself matters.

## PERFECT THE POWER INTRO

**The BADASS knows how to create engagement and intrigue.**

Introductions are tough. What question does everyone ask? "What do you do?" Have you ever introduced yourself with "I am a <title>" or "I sell <product>" only to receive a lukewarm reception? Never introduce yourself by your title or the product you sell. The goal of any introduction is to initiate conversation. If you are looking to make a powerful introduction it should include some of the following elements:

- **Differentiate Yourself as a *Specialist, Expert or Professional*:** It increases your credibility and authority.
- **Always Use Your First and Last Names:** It improves the receiver's ability to remember and it is perceived as more powerful, professional, projecting greater impact.
- **Something that creates intrigue, interest, humor:** It gets them asking questions. I often say "I create UNSTOPPABLE BADASS SUPERSTARS."

- **Include Areas of Differentiation:** What makes you, your product or your company special or unique? What skills or service do you deliver that make you stand out from your competition, or provides an additional service or benefit to the client?

- **The Big Benefit:** Be sure to communicate the big benefit or end result that they will receive as a result of using your product or service.

***"Hi, I am <First Name Last Name> a <Professional>… <Creates impact, humor, intrigue, leaves them asking for more>***

***We work with <Type of Customer> and specialize in***

***<Point of Differentiation/Outcome #1> and***

***<Point of Differentiation/Outcome #2> so they can***

***<Big Benefit>.***

**"Hi, I am John Brown, a Real Estate Professional with ABC Company.**

***We make movers into stress-free shakers!***

**We specialize in working with recently transferred business Executives,**

**providing them with value-add services such as no-charge home packing services and free moving trucks**

**so they can have a stress-free moving experience.**

That is much more interesting and informative than "Hi, I am John Brown. I am a realtor with ______." Leave the blah-blah-blah behind and come up with a statement that intrigues and engages your prospect, leaving them wanting to know more.

**TIP: Use language that stands out. Use unique adjectives and adverbs (description words) to create more impact, i.e. catapult sales instead of increase sales.**

Remember, your goal is to start a conversation. A good intro intrigues them, tells them who you work with, what you do, how you are different, and why they should be talking to you. You may need multiple power intros depending on who you are talking to. Memorize them.

**TIP: The most effective and powerful introductions are the ones kept closest to ten words, two sentences maximum, so that others can easily recite and repeat.**

## NAIL YOUR NETWORKING

**The BADASS knows the power of networking is the secret to today's business growth.**

What better way to get others to know you and trust you than to meet and talk with them in an environment that encourages conversation, builds rapport and relationships. Whether you attend formal networking events, professional associations, industry meetings, trade shows, personal interest groups, or social events, all are opportunities to get to know people and create a well-established circle of supporters and referrals. Developing new relationships is an essential part of business today and BADASS SUPERSTARS do it on a regular basis. It may not show immediate results, but it can eventually lead to an open door or opportunity for new business.

As Wendy Going from Timber Tech Truss candidly said:

> ***"I am usually too busy to meet with people unless I know them. That is why you need to be out networking, working hard and hustling to build relationships, trust and a reputation. And it takes time."***

I have always maximized my networking opportunities. My ability to refer, connect and introduce others has been an incredible benefit throughout my career and people regularly come to me for information, recommendations or referrals.

> **TIP: Network events are a fabulous way to meet new people but be conscientious of your time and the quality of attendees at these events. They should be filled with your target Avatars. Remember, your time is money.**

Do not meet someone and right away ask them for coffee. People see right through that. Instead try to have several non-selling touch points where you can set the foundation for a relationship, getting to know them a little first. Get their contact info, provide value items, invite them to a network event, anything but going straight for the coffee. Educate, do not aggravate.

## BUSINESS CARDS STILL MATTER

**BADASS SUPERSTARS understand the endless benefits business cards bring.**

Follow up any introduction with a good business card. The type of card you have reflects who you are just as much as a powerful introduction. Logos mean very little unless you are a global brand. Focus needs to be in messaging what it is you deliver to those using your services. Put all your contact info with a meaningful tagline on one side, with the services you provide on the back. Look at your card. Does it tell people exactly what you do? Give it to a stranger and ask them. Unfortunately, so many do not directly relay the message we think our cards project. Remember, this is your advertising, especially if you are a solopreneur.

A photo should be used when you are providing a service; real estate, insurance, financial. multi-level marketing. Ensure it has a meaningful tagline and on the back, list the key service you provide. If you do provide a photo, put a current one on. In today's selling where authenticity and credibility are so important, using a photo from 20 years ago looks deceptive, damaging your professionalism and integrity.

A business card is still the most effective direct marketing tool you will ever have. It is the first and lasting impression of the company. It is a hardcopy reminder, an advertisement and brand awareness generator. And most importantly, it creates numerous touch points, keeping you top-of-mind. Every time the receiver sees it or touches it, it becomes a reminder of you. But remember, it needs to be updated regularly. If it looks like an old dated design, what does that say about you and your business?

## TIPS:

- **Business cards go through trends like anything else. Weight, colour, design, print and format change. Check with your printer to find out what is the latest and greatest design.**
- **The thicker the card stock, the more professional the impression. It feels expensive and projects the same.**

I have always used two types of business cards. The regular ones for handing out to customers, and a peel and stick one for materials. My team and I would put our cards on every product catalogue, binder and piece of literature. Regular business cards can fall off, get lost or misplaced over time. The peel and stick ones stay on forever. In fact, I left American Standard a number of years ago, yet I still receive inquiries as a result of those cards.

A common practice these days is to give people numerous cards to use as referral cards. They know a happy customer will gladly give them away, with a positive word-of-mouth referral, spreading the word to others.

Professionalism is projected when you have business cards on hand at events. With word-of-mouth referrals being so influential, why would anyone go empty-handed? How many potential opportunities are missed by not having cards? What do those missed occasions equate to in lost income?

Digitally exchanging contact information is efficient, but unfortunately, it is impersonal and lacks future touch point opportunities. Networking and making genuine relationships are priorities in modern selling, cards help facilitate those connections.

We have all been guilty of forgetting our cards at one time or another, but the key is to have that little backup stash ready to go. Where can you put them; your car, gym bag, residence-front door, computer bag, luggage?

And even if there is no business or referral to come from that valuable little card, it is always a great conversation starter.

# TIPS:

- **Always reach out with "a great to meet you" within 24 hours. Connect on the social networks and enter the info into your CRM.**
- **There are some great card scanning apps available. I use CARD CAM. You line it up, it takes and picture. It downloads into your phone and creates a database that can be transferred into your Outlook or CRM.**

## MEET AND GREET INTROS

**The BADASS will ask for help getting introductions and meeting people.**

With word of mouth being so important, the most efficient and successful way to build your network today is to ask for referral introductions. Asking your current customers for referrals is a good habit, but it isn't enough. Reach out to all your past clients, friends, associates and personal contacts and ask them to introduce you to someone in their circle. Kieran Longworth, Recruiter at LOCK SEARCH GROUP, states:

> ***"Today it is important that salespeople are well networked. Who they know and the strength of their relationships within their customer base is as important, as what they know."***

Also, if you are looking to meet the decision maker at a particular company, don't be afraid to ask for an introduction from people who work there. The sales representatives often have a lot more influence than you realize.

Ask them if it is okay to use their name when contacting the prospect. Or better yet, ask them for a face-to-face introduction or send the decision maker an email introduction including you and your contact information. This is the most effective way to meet new clients today.

Do not name drop if you do not have a solid relationship with the person. I did this as a rookie, at my couch potato job. Big mistake. I walked out embarrassed and humiliated. Ugh!

# GIVE THE BEST GIFT EVER

**A BADASS knows a referral is the best gift you can give a customer.**

Refer their business to others. When we contact a customer, too often we are trying to get something from them. Instead, be of service to them. The ultimate act of servitude would be to send your client a new customer. You helped them increase their sales, which is what everyone needs and can always use more of… and you thought enough of them—that you provided the priceless, word-of-mouth referral. It will gain you tremendous respect and loyalty.

## Law of Reciprocity

Psychologists believe that deeply rooted in the human psyche is a social norm that drives to respond to a positive action with an equal, if not greater positive reaction. This process is called reciprocity. Based on the eye for an eye principle, reciprocity is an unconscious and automatic reaction that triggers feelings of indebtedness. There are two types of reciprocity:

**Emotional Reciprocity:**

- **If you make me feel good, I want to make you feel good.**
- **If you make me feel good, I will make you feel good by buying your product.**

**Physical Reciprocity:**

- **If you do something nice for me,**
- **I will do something nice for you.**

It is human nature that people do not like to owe others. This is why companies give away schwag; clothing, mugs, trips, tours etc. Yes, their logos are on these products to promote the brand, but more so it is a reminder to the person receiving the gift, that they were deemed as special in the eyes of the company. The company in turn, hopes that the reciprocity will take place, leading to future purchasing.

Finding ways to do kindnesses and favours for your clients, will only strengthen the relationship. But keep in mind, it needs to be a genuine and authentic act of kindness, not a manipulative one.

# CHAPTER 5

# Prospect To PROFIT

**A BADASS perseveres and understands the meaning of tenacity.**

Maximize your sales opportunities by using all prospecting methods available; telephone, email, website and social media. Remember consistency and providing value are essential.

We had recently moved back to the city after living up north in a remote town for my husband's career. We had moved back with no jobs and needed to find work right away. I was presented with an offer as a District Manager for a large cosmetics company. There were many benefits; a move up the career ladder, a great title, a company car, flexible hours, the ability to work from home, and work with a wonderful group of ladies. I was so excited.

I was hired to oversee a group of sales ladies—most of whom originated as stay at home moms. Few, if any, had a true sales background, but they did have the right attitude plus strong friend and family networks to work with. Each month, I would do a big sales meeting teaching them how to improve their sales and expand their cosmetic knowledge. I encouraged them to be themselves, be empathetic, treat others the way they would like to be treated, implement my sales methodologies and to prepare-prepare-prepare. Their confidence and sales numbers excelled.

It is funny how the universe presents you with what you "need" in life, not necessarily what you want? The real challenge in this role was the requirement to find and hire three to four new independent consultants per week! Yes, per week. More than eighty to ninety per cent of this job was straight cold calling! The Regional Manager made it perfectly clear that if we didn't bring new sales representatives weekly and reach our numbers, we would lose our jobs. No, not admired in today's standard of leadership, but believe me, her method worked. I desperately needed this job and the income it provided.

Company training consisted of asking open-ended versus closed-ended questions (closed-ended can be answered with a yes or a no and kills your conversation) and a reverse directory.

I was assigned a district in the south end of the city. I believed I could do it, but that awkward uncomfortable feeling reared its ugly head again. I had responsibilities that I couldn't shirk. I HAD to be successful at this. I started with telling myself, "I can do this" and "Take action, keep moving forward." Reciting these positive manifestations gave me the courage to go from full out fear, to a state of terrifying trepidation.

Day after day, I would make a huge list of people to contact. Then I picked up the phone and called. I pushed through my anxiety. And I just kept doing it. Difficult at first as I was wracked with that old familiar feeling of dejection each and every time, I spoke to someone. I stumbled and fumbled my way through at first. I didn't like it, but I knew that if I kept at it and kept forcing myself to make those calls, I would be okay. I relied on staying positive and optimistic. I expected the worst in terms of understanding most of the calls would end in a NO, but for fun, I kept score and made it a game.

To my surprise, the more I did it, the better I became, and the positive results started to show. I made a point of celebrating the wins which kept me inspired and motivated. My attitude moved from anxious to relaxed and jovial.

I created a two-sentence power intro, "Hi, ding-dong Avon calling.... I am Jackie Rainforth. We specialize in helping women feel radiant and beautiful, while enabling them to earn extra money for the added things they want for their families. What special thing would you want for your family?" The 'ding-dong' them laugh and immediately lowered their resistance. ('Ding-Dong Avon calling'... was from a highly identifiable Marketing and Ad campaign that Avon had done.) While the remainder of the power statement captured their attention, prompting them to answer and expand on their dreams for the family. Most importantly, it started a conversation, resulting in them asking me more about the program. Each morning I would get up, put my brave face on, and make my calls without stopping. Funny thing... I started to get faster results. It became very natural and genuine, an easy conversation between two people. In eleven months, I tripled the number of sales representatives and the territory went from the 128th position out of 130 in Canada, to #1 in Alberta and #3 in Canada!

And the best part is that I had triumphantly conquered my fear of cold calling! I was incredibly proud! You can't imagine how great it was to go from "couch surfer" to receiving accolades and awards. And as an additional bonus, I discovered a phenomenal system for cold calling!

# PROPEL YOUR PROSPECTING

**THE BADASS knows how to use their time wisely.**

Good time management is about taking the time to prospect, making it a prioritized task that demands your full attention. It is about organizing your day, week or month, to ensure you set aside the time to get it done, with the long-term goal of becoming an automated habit.

Commit to setting aside a few hours every week to call contacts on your list. The old adage "time is money" is true. Regular prospecting will keep your sales funnel full and grow your business. It is likely the most valuable time you will ever spend as a salesperson. But remember, make sure your prospecting is targeted.

# KNOW YOUR AVATAR

**THE BADASS takes the time to understand every aspect of his client.**

Knowing and understanding your 'avatar', target market or ideal customer will help you achieve faster results in your business and help you improve your time management by avoiding wasting time making calls on prospects who may or may not be looking for your product and service. Better to focus your efforts on a narrowly defined 'ideal' group who will have higher odds of creating a positive impact on your business.

1. **Define their Specific Demographics:** Write down everything you can about what the characteristics and parameters of who that ideal client would be. For example, is it a Business or Individual? Annual revenue? Corporation or privately owned? Number of Employees? Occupation? Gender? Age? Ethnicity? Community?

Look at the characteristics of your current clientele to help you determine your ideal market.

2. **Define the Specific Problems, Challenges and Needs:** What do you think your target market desperately needs? What issues or challenges do you think are universal in your industry? What services are your competitors currently providing and what needs are they fulfilling? Where do you think the gaps are?

3. **Define the Fringe Prospects:** Call on and exhaust your leads with your 'ideal' clients before you move onto the 'fringe' prospects. Again, look for the gaps. Do they have the same challenges, issues and needs as your ideal clients? If so, who is servicing them? And why? If not, decide if there is a path worth pursuing?

## A REALLY BIG LIST

**A BADASS SUPERSTAR recognizes the importance of hunting.**

Go online to find new potential prospects that you have researched and qualified. Write down the contact info and names of as many potential prospects as you can.

- Go through the old file of potential leads that you have been ignoring but have been meaning to get to.
- Make a list of old contacts and past customers that you can reach out to and ask, "do you know anyone?", or better yet ask for an introduction.
- Make a really big list; hundreds, thousands, tens of thousands.
- Spend your career building a database.

The good news, with advancement of artificial intelligence, big data and its advanced statistical power and high complexity will be a welcome transformation to the sales industry. The mundane tasks of tracking and creating lists will one day be laid to rest.

For now, know that five or ten names are not enough to keep you going and ward off the dejection that comes with prospecting. Having a long list increases your odds of success and helps you overcome the fear that often comes with cold calling. Once you have that list, start calling and do not stop. The more you do, the more comfortable it will become. A short list enables one to give up too quickly.

## THE GATEKEEPER

**BADASS SUPERSTARS treat everyone with equal respect.**

It is the Gatekeeper's job to filter out the calls and control access to the decision maker. Make them your friend, they can provide valuable information. You want to learn more about the company and the specifics of their situation, find out who the decision maker is plus their cell phone number and the best time to call.

- **Respect:** You never know who the Gatekeeper is. They could be the wife, the daughter, the niece of the CEO or owner. I have had that job and it is not an easy one. Always treat them with the utmost respect and do not forget them.

One holiday season when I worked as a receptionist, a certain FedEx driver who was always incredibly kind stopped in and gave me a beautifully wrapped gift. A tiny, beautifully wrapped box with two delicious pieces of a luxury brand chocolate. It was the smallest of gestures, an act of kindness which I am sure they did for everyone, but in that moment, I felt special. It was never forgotten. A small act of reciprocity that sits deep in the recesses of my mind. To this day, FedEx is still my preferred courier provider.

**TIP: Selling focus should always be from the customer perspective. How will this make my customer feel? Remember, people buy on emotion first, then use logic to support.**

- **Ask for Help:** Start with "I was wondering if you could help me." Asking for help rarely gets turned down.

**TIP: If you can, also get to know the Salesperson at the company you are interested in and trying to gain access to, as they are typically big influencers within the organization.**

- **Ask Open-Ended Questions to Gain Access to Decision Maker:** Ask an array of questions to find out as much as you can about the decision maker, the company, and the specifics of their situation: "I am trying to find the best person to talk to with regards to ________________________. Who would you suggest that be?" and, "What would be the best way to contact them?", "Can you please confirm what time (decision maker) is typically in and what time they usually leave?" "Is there something they particularly appreciate when seeing salespeople?", "Do they have a favourite activity, sport or team?", "Is there anyone else involved in the decision-making process", "Who is your current supplier?" "Do you believe the decision-maker would be open to looking at…?"

All these questions can provide valuable information that can assist you in with the decision-maker later on.

# THE OLD-FASHIONED TELEPHONE CALL

**The BADASS SUPERSTAR knows perseverance.**

What was once old is now new again! Few people are using the telephone, preferring instead to send emails… but surprise, surprise, that the old phone is gaining momentum as a mode for prospecting. Two statistics to keep in mind:

***"The average business person receives 113 emails daily."***

—Radicati Group

***"Only 24% of all emails is opened."***

—Resourceful Selling

It is, in fact, one of the most effective ways to gain new customers. Here are some pleasantly astonishing facts:

***"Fifty-seven per cent of C-level buyers prefer that salespeople call them."***

—Rain Group

***"Fifty-nine per cent of buyers accepted a call from new salespeople in the past 12 months."***

—Resource Selling

***"Eighty-two of buyers accept meetings when salespeople reach out to them."***

—Rain Group

Good news! Scientists say that passion, tone and pauses are crucial and tell us a lot about the communication we are having, much more so than the printed word. So, let's pick up that phone!

## Practice What You Will Say

THE BADASS SUPERSTARS are fully prepared before they dial. They know what they are going to say, how they are going to say it, what their goal and purpose of the phone call is, they are polished in their speech (no mentions of so, uhm and ah, please) they practice a couple trial runs before calling, and they have their resources (documents, schedule and things they want to say) within reach. Their notebooks and pens are ready to take notes!

**TIP: Call yourself and leave the message you would like to leave with the decision maker. How do you sound? Do you need improvement or are you ready to start bringing in new customers? Repetition is the key to mastery.**

## The Best Time to Call

Phone early in the morning or late at the end of the day and NEVER ON A TUESDAY. Your phone call will have a much better chance of being responded to if you can phone before the hustle and bustle of the day gets going.

Tuesdays are the busiest day of the week. Most people spend Monday getting organized for the week. Tuesdays, their heads are buried, and the last thing they have time for is discussing new products or services. Statistics show WEDNESDAYS and THURSDAYS are best, they were found to be 24.9% better than the worst day (Lead Response Management Study). Personally, I find Fridays are also a great day as people are winding down and more relaxed.

The same study reveals C-Suite and Senior Executives will answer calls around 6:30 a.m. because they are early risers and maximize productivity with an early start (Harvard Business

Review/Nawaz). But tread lightly, you do not want to anger your prospect because you called too early. You had better make sure this is a viable course of action, by clarifying the habits of the decision maker with the Gatekeeper first.

## Leaving a Message

When you leave a message, talk slowly and clearly. Nervousness tends to make us speed up. Then take a couple deep breaths before you call, it will assist you in slowing down your speech, increasing the effectiveness of your communication. Keep it simple with the content focused on them and the potential value you can bring to the table. Each message should be slightly different.

Wendy Going, GM Calgary Division/Managing Partner for Timber Tech Truss advises:

***"Always call to set up an appointment.<br>Never ever show up at someone's office without an appointment. This allows you client to make time in their busy schedule to accommodate a productive discussion with you.<br>Be respectful of your customer's busy schedule."***

## Meaningful Voice Mail

A good voice mail is well-planned, spoken clearly and confidently, sparks interest and it prompts the prospect to call you back. Do not rush to describe your product and why it would be a perfect fit for your prospect nor how they should take action now. Selling is about meeting the customer's needs. Ideally, the message should be short and compelling. It needs to capture their attention and want them asking for more information. You want them to be intrigued and captivated, wanting more information.

You must be super persistent and tenacious when making cold calls. Being personally prepared with the ability to push through, keep going, and continuously take action are mandatory mindsets in overcoming the fear that comes with prospecting. My rules of thumb:

- **Phone at Least Three Times:** Good salespeople know that persistence is a measure that executives can and will often use to rate the importance of a call, and the professionalism of a salesperson. Call at least three to six times, a week apart, stressing the value you can provide and the outcome they can expect.

***"44% of Sales Reps give up after one follow-up call."***

—Brevet

- **Leave your Name, Company Name and Phone number:** Speak clearly, and slowly and repeat again at the end of the message. There is nothing more frustrating than having to go through the process of listening to a message numerous times because you were not able to catch it the first time. On a cold call it is best to simply leave your name and phone number evoking curiosity.

**TIP: Superstars know that they should repeat their full name and number twice. Repeating it is a common courtesy to the receiver.**

## Busy or Ghosted?

The advancement of technology and communication products such as call display, voice mail and email, have made accessing decision-makers more difficult, as people can avoid salespeople by hiding behind technology.

> ***"For salespeople, it now takes an average of eight cold call attempts to reach a prospect or make a first appointment versus a decade ago when it was only three or four."***
>
> —Harvard Business School

It is difficult to know whether they are busy, or they are simply ghosting you—simply refusing to return your calls. Unfortunately, you will not know unless you leave a series of messages. I usually leave up to six approximately one week apart:

**MESSAGE #1:** Let them know that you have checked them out and have done your homework. Say something like: "I read your LinkedIn profile and a number of articles on your company", then lead into the Power Introduction and the value you can provide.

**INTRO:** ***"Hi I am <Name> with <Company>."***

**VALUE:** ***"After researching, we believe we can... reduce/improve your...***

**PROOF:** ***"We have assisted many clients with this exact issue and have accumulated numerous testimonials and reviews on the same issue."***

**CONTACT:** ***"We would love to see if we are a fit and or our product makes sense for You and your Organization. Please call me back at <phone #>."***

**REPEAT:** ***"Again, my name is <Name> my contact number is <Phone>."***

**MESSAGE #2:** Lightly touch on how you can help them achieve their goals:

***"I believe we have a product or service that could be of interest and help you… I am not trying to sell you something, but rather, find out if it applies to your situation, and whether it would be a good fit for your situation."***

This moves it from selling to more of a conversation.

**MESSAGE #3:** Try to arrange a short conversation 48 hours later:

***"Would you have fifteen minutes to have a quick discussion to see if our product/service is a good fit and makes sense for you/your Organization? I would greatly appreciate the opportunity as I believe it could potentially offer some significant benefits."***

**MESSAGE #4:** People do not return phone calls because they are incredibly busy. Often it is not because they do not want to talk to you, they simply do not have the time. Be direct and to the point:

***"I have reached out a number of times, and since this might not be the right time to connect, I do not want to bother you. Please give me a quick call, I will not take up more than five minutes of your time. I believe you will find it very worthwhile."***

**MESSAGE #5:** Pick a negative issue or challenges that you believe your client might have and quickly touch on how your product or service could provide the resolution/value they need, hoping now is the right time to get together. Reach out again, ask:

***"Many of clients in your field experience…
I truly believe we can save/help you... Is there a reason for hesitancy or are there any concerns you would like to discuss? Again, I will only take up five minutes of your time. Please let me know if you would like us to stop contacting you."***

**MESSAGE #6:** By this point, chances are they really do not want to talk to you—but keep going until you hear a NO. Persistence pays.

***"I understand this is not the right time for you, but please note I am here to help. If you need anything, please feel free to call."***

Keep reaching out on a monthly basis but shift to sending value-add or educational items.

**TIP: Send an item of personal interest (based on what you learned from the gatekeeper). I once sent a client an aviation clock, because I knew the prospect loved flying. He loved it! And of course, make sure your card is attached.**

**Remember:**

- **"New to Market" Products:** These take longer to sell and can take up to 32% more cold calls to get through to decision makers.
- **Respect the NO:** If the prospect says NO, respect it. Do not try to force a sales pitch, get angry, or become defiant. You can have another customer somewhere else.
- **Always thank them for their time:** This is common courtesy that shows professionalism.

Prospecting can be tough but keep the right mindset and do not take it personally. If you can regularly schedule time to prospect (preferably in the morning before your day gets going), a couple days per week, you will keep your pipeline full. And eventually, a remarkable thing will happen—your business will start to grow organically through referrals and word of mouth.

**TIP: Your number one priority, regardless of where you are in your business, is to prospect and keep your pipeline full.**

**IMPORTANT TIPS:**

- If you do not have a steady revenue stream (new business or new sales representative) 65% of your time should be spent prospecting and making connections. Focus needs to be on growing your business.
- Always focus on warm leads not cold calls. A warm lead, you have received a referral, you have recently met the person, or they have requested information or opted-in through social media, are the types of leads that often have higher success rates.

## DIGITAL PROSPECTING AND CRM

**The BADASS jumps on and rides the shift into the future.**

You have a few options when it comes to digital prospecting. One, write a direct email sent with a specific person in mind, or a mass email that is more generalized. Create a database from all the business cards you have collected over the years (including past and present customers) opt-ins from social media and any new potential prospects.

Or there are a number of automated email campaign services, such as MailChimp or Constant Contact that you can use to set up a series of email. Remember, you need to receive their permission to market/contact due to strict privacy laws. When customers volunteer their email through an online opt-in form, or hand you their business card, they have given you their permission. Every email should have the option to opt-out or unsubscribe so they can de-list at any time.

## Direct Email

Use your database to send information to a targeted and specific set of potential prospects. The important to-do here is personalize, making it relevant and of interest. Do the following:

- **Use the Person's Name:** Use the person's name to personalize the email.
- **Include Three Pain Point Questions to Start:** A great way to capture their attention is to start with questions identifying three common pain points or challenges, written as headlines. For example:
    - **Do You Stay Up at Night Worrying About…?**
    - **Are You Constantly Faced With…?**
    - **Do You Wish…?**
- **Power Introduction:** Include the information from your Power Intro; how you, your company and your product differentiate from others in the market, and the benefits you provide. Loss aversion is best.
- **Make it Personal:** Use names whenever possible and (or) make the content relevant to the recipient

- **Keep the Content Short:** Remember… people have a very short attention span and only glance at things these days.
- **Point Form:** Other than your introduction and conclusion paragraphs, keep things in bullet form whenever possible, with a maximum of 3-5 points as it is easier to read.
- **Testimonial:** This is a great place to include a testimonial.
- **Schedule a Follow Up:** Let them know you will be following up and when. Then make sure you do. It should be done within a week or so from them receiving your email.
- **Include a Follow Up Takeaway Piece:** A piece of literature with your card attached, a sample or a gift serve as reminders, and create interest.

## Opt-In Email Wave

Mass email marketing has evolved from the untargeted, spam-like shots in the dark, to finely-tuned email automation programs and strategies. They are personalized, have purpose, value and relevancy. Engagement levels and reach have escalated due to personalized segmentation, dynamic content, abandon cart functions, and big data retrieval. Instead of being a one-way transaction, the person opting in often receives something of value in return. It is a boomerang cycle with a massive reach. The goal today is to create brand recognition and engagement through connectivity opportunity, hopefully and ultimately benefiting in a sale. However, bear in mind that the data and contact information retrieved from the interaction is nearly as important. Whether you go all out with an automated system, or use your internal or personal database, keep the following in mind:

- **Make It an Easy Read:** Keep content short in efforts to make it easy to read. With shorter attention spans, bullet form is often best.
- **Deliver Valuable Information:** If doing a generalized mass mail out, be sure to provide value-based content (tips, newsletters, quotes, e-books etc.) to educate and entice.
- **Be Consistent:** Consistency is the key. If you send a newsletter, do it monthly.
- **Photo and Contact Info:** Make sure your photo/logo is included. All contact information, website and social media links so they can check you out further.
- **Call to Action:** Include a "call to action" at the end of the content. What is it you want them to do next? It could be something as simple as "Please call for more information", "Forward this to receive", "Watch this video" "Complete this…"
- **Request a Referral:** End with asking for a referral. "Referrals are our biggest compliment. Who do you know that might be interested in our product/services?" and possibly provide an incentive for doing so "Receive a free…"
- **Sign Up with Marketing Software like Mailchimp and Constant Connect:** This way, you can automate and improve consistency and engagement rates.

As technology changes, the role of email in marketing continues to expand and become more sophisticated. As we move into the future, I believe it will continue to be a very viable way to prospect.

***"Email marketing provides an average ROI of $44 for every $1 spent. Eighty-six per cent of B2B Marketers use email campaigns to generate new opportunities and handle business."***

—Snap

## SOCIAL MEDIA BUTTERFLY

**Today's BADASS understands the importance of a personal brand.**

Social media tools are a powerful and advantageous way to find new prospects, gain referrals and expand overall market reach, especially for those who have limited budgets and no opportunity for advertising or access to a sales team.

Only 44% of top sales performers are using social networks when researching prospects (HubSpot). This is mandatory today as gaining valuable insight into a prospect's interests, background, trigger points and career history will help you to personalize their experience and maximize your outreach efforts. An astonishing 50 million small businesses have recognized the benefits and are using Facebook Pages to connect with their customers.

## CREATE A PERSONAL BRAND

**The BADASS knows that a personal brand = network and business opportunities.**

Growing numbers of salespeople are also maximizing their opportunities through social networks by establishing online personal brands. They are reaching masses, establishing themselves as experts in an area. I have done this on LinkedIn. I post five times a week and do a weekly "Sales Tip by The Rainmaker" video. I have created an immense following as a result.

***"Video is 40 times likely to get shared on social media than any other type of content."***

—The Brevet Group

Branding yourself is important as the buyer wants to be able to investigate and get to know their salesperson before committing to them. People want to see a more personal side to you—your values, thoughts, family, areas of importance like sport, interests where people can identify with you and feel like they can get to know you better.

Post relevant industry content, shared interests and topics that start a conversation, as well as promoting company-sponsored content.

***"Seventy-eight per cent of salespeople using social media outsell their peers!"***

—The Brevet Group

Yes, if you are not doing it, you are being left behind. If you are leading a sales team, you need to get yourself and your team up to speed. The result; a larger network, stronger sales relationships, the creation and reinforcement of trust, extended credibility and authority, familiarity, generation of leads and referrals, and increase customer loyalty. For many, this will be pushing your comfort zone, but once you start doing it, you will be amazed at the benefits it generates.

***"Half of the revenue is influenced by social selling."***

—Hubspot

Discover the social media platforms that best meet your target market and concentrate on keeping them up to date. Again, this is how Millennials determine trust. If you have your own social media brand and presence, Millennials will feel like they know you, like you, and will ultimately trust and buy from you.

> **TIP: The ideal time to post is 7 a.m., 11 a.m. and 5 p.m. during the week. (Lead Management Study)**

Shane Wenzel, President of one of Alberta's largest residential construction companies, SHANE HOME GROUP OF COMPANIES was one of the first visionary trendsetter social media experts, years before anyone really knew what social media was. He had a lot of pushback from people within his organization as they thought he was wasting time and money. They certainly do not think that any more. Today, he encourages people to build their own brands and jump onboard with social selling because it is the new and modern way to network, build relationships and increase your exposure:

***"Do the same on social media as you would in life. Introduce yourself, have a conversation, make a connection and hopefully, they will eventually become a buyer. It is the electronic version of networking. It is okay if you throw out the occasional advertisement, but it is about building on-line relationships."***

Putting yourself *out there* takes a lot of courage.

I remember the day my social media person suggested I do a weekly video. I was like "NO WAY!" Why in the world would I want to go from the comfortable state of anonymity, to open myself up to criticism, condemnation and judgement in a recorded and forever format for the world to see? The concept was beyond terrifying. Yes, that old friend named Fear, was back. I opened my mind, changed the internal dialogue, and pushed through the stall wall. I put my first video out there a couple years ago. It was painful! And I'm sure equally painful to watch. I must have re-taped it a hundred times. I was filled with anxiety as I hit the post button. I had to change my thought process.

Instead of focusing on the negative, I chose to look at the positive. I remind myself that the process is totally worthwhile if I can help one person out there feel more confident and self-assured through the sharing of my knowledge and experience. I have changed the inner dialogue making it about others rather than myself, and it has become much easier to do. As my audience and views increased, I am still shocked when I run into people who tell me they like my videos and I have helped them. Wow! Those moments make all the anxiety and nervousness worth it.

# CHAPTER 6

# Differentiate To ELEVATE

**The BADASS leaves uniformity to the Competition.** If there is one thing that salespeople and companies need to do in today's highly competitive and resistant market, it is to create distinction and unique selling positions. Differentiating ourselves, our companies, products and services, will be the driving force moving forward. We must up our game, serve more, deliver more, and become value-add partners helping to advise and support our customers and their businesses in the evolution of their growth. As Keith Strachan, General Manager for Wolselely Canada Inc., a man with tremendous business acumen and insight, eloquently states:

***"Today it is about the customer experience and bringing value. You need to save them money, make them money, and provide solutions – what is their pain point and how are you going to solve it? Our goal is to help our chosen partners succeed and we believe it should be enjoyable to do business with us – we believe in doing it together."***

We are most certainly in critical and challenging times. Look for the gaps that exist and capitalize on them. What can you do that sets you apart from product and service providers in your industry to gain a competitive advantage?

## PRODUCT DIFFERENTIATION

**The BADASS knows that success is measured by how well one can differentiate.**

When your product or service is unique and stands alone, the perception is that no other can compete.

I used to be the Regional Sales Manager for a company called In-Sink-Erator, overseeing a number of salespeople and independent sales agencies. We sold garbage disposals for kitchen sinks. We would be up against a lower priced competitive line regularly.

When I started with the company, I did a thorough research of both product lines. What I discovered was that In-Sink-Erator had this very cool accessory called a Sink-Top-Switch. It was a fancy air pump switch that installed in the countertop and easily turn the unit on and off, maximizing kitchen efficiency. Prior to its introduction, one would have to open the counter cupboard door under the sink and find the electrical switch to operate. I knew immediately that this was a gem because of its convenience.

> **TIP: Empathy is essential in selling. Always put yourself in your customer's shoes, and think "What would my response to this product, service or situation be?"**

We started to promote the garburator and the switch as a paired or bundled product line in our presentations. Within no time, we were able to get it into stock and on display everywhere. My hunch (and research) was right. I had found a product gap and capitalized on it, as the other company didn't have the same product offering.

**TIP: Bundling products together is a great way to increase sales.**

As a result of our ability to differentiate and sell the value of the disposal WITH the bonus of the Sink-Top-Switch, our sales skyrocketed taking it from a non-existent product in the market place to one that is still a top-selling item. Our total sales increased by over 30% and of course, our overall market share and brand rose to even higher heights.

**TIP: Adding a bonus discount or product will attract those looking for a bargain and increase the sale.**

As we did with the Sink-Top-Switch, if your product knowledge is impeccable, not only can you navigate through the strengths and weaknesses to your benefit; sometimes you can find a gap that leaves your competition out in the cold.

**TIP: ALWAYS look for creative new ways to stay ahead of the pack, as competition will quickly copy your success.**

## KNOWLEDGE DIFFERENTIATION

**The BADASS knows the more you learn, the more you earn.**

Understanding the competitor product can be invaluable because it allows you to differentiate by focusing on your strengths over theirs.

When I was with Kohler Canada Inc., a global luxury plumbing line, I realized that never have I worked for a company that had done such an amazing—and I do mean amazing—job of onboarding and employee education and development. Hired as a Sales Rep to do handle their Builder and Showroom sales for the Province, they flew me down to Kohler Wisconsin for product training. I was expecting the standard training in a classroom environment. We toured the manufacturing plants to see how everything was made. That in itself was incredible, but was I ever surprised when we arrived at the engineering lab. Not only did we learn the fundamentals of all our products, we also learned about the competitor products. We were given tools and instructed to take the products apart noticing the construction and quality. Then they instructed us to rebuild it and install it. Wow! We did this with tubs, faucets, toilets and all the competitor lines.

**TIP: Seek out help from as many experts or peers as you can to help give you a better understanding and perspective of how a product, service, market, and the competition operates. The best learning is often the takeaways from others.**

Talk about getting a firsthand understanding of the differences and the impact those differences would make out in the field! A phenomenal experience from numerous perspectives, we understood ease of installation, product quality and value price comparison! And it gets better.

Each year, they would fly all the sales staff back to Kohler for training sessions with the product managers. A product manager is the person who designs, creates and brings the item to fruition. They were the people who had an intimate understanding of the engineering, testing, marketing and market value of the product based on the complete thought processes behind the introduction of the product.

**TIP: Consistent learning and development is crucial. If your company does not provide, do so for yourself by reaching out to others or enrolling in learning and development opportunities. Employers seek out new hires with continuous and proactive education.**

When we hit the streets selling the line, we knew everything there was to know. By giving us such in-depth training, we knew the products inside and out. We were able to promote the products before their release, elevating pre-sales hype and desire, so that when the launch took place, there was healthy demand and support behind it.

**TIP: Thorough product knowledge will help you excel in selling because you will be more confident in educating the customer.**

Kohler understood the value of product differentiation. My product knowledge combined with my sales skills and ability to cold call enabled me to grow my territory sales over 60% and I was named #1 succession performer for Canada. Thorough product knowledge differentiation made me a force to be reckoned with! I was a BADASS.

## PRICE DIFFERENTIATION

**The BADASS SUPERSTARS embraces uniqueness.**

One needs to know how to outsell their competition and increase their market share by strategically distinguishing their products and services from others selling similar items, without getting into a price war.

When you have a commodity or generic item where all the features and benefits are the same as your competitor's, the only area of differentiation between you is price. This becomes an advanced challenge. Relying on price alone is not a good selling strategy because someone always comes along and lowers their price, typically erupting into a price war. Trying to compete this way is bad business. It demolishes margins and undermines the industry. This happened when I was representing American Standard.

A basic entry level, commodity item was priced at $100 per unit for years. As other commodity lines would enter the marketplace the competition would drop their price in efforts to gain market share and vie for an advantage. Within no time, the price had deteriorated to $60/unit, a rock bottom price for all. They kept dropping until the entire market had eroded, turning what was once a very profitable product into a loss leader with zero profitability.

Too often, I see entrepreneurs get into price wars with their competitors because they do not know how to "value-solution" sell. Learn to sell by highlighting the differences between your product and service and theirs. Or find a strategic way to be creative in your selling.

Again, at American Standard, we sold luxury lines like Jado and Porcher. Many of the small boutiques would carry the same manufacturers products as they were not large enough to gain exclusivity through mass purchasing and distribution agreements. All would be selling the same products at the same prices, making it difficult to compete because their customers would shop around for the best price. They knew that lowering the price on the product would kill the profitability of the sale and drive the market into the ground. So instead, one of the boutiques came up with a creative solution that put them ahead of the others. Not one the manufacturers were fond of it, but it worked.

The boutique would change out the displays to a different size and color, remove the logos and branding, and assign their own names and codes to the each of the products in the lineup, eliminating the potential for their customers to compare and price shop. A lot of work yes, but brilliant in terms of maintaining their profit margins, and the integrity of the product in the marketplace.

> **TIP: Always seek out ways to differentiate from your competition in efforts to protect or grow market share and potentially ask for a higher price.**

It was outside of the box thinking used to outsell their competitors and maintain their price and profitability. Brilliant.

## PROCESS DIFFERENTIATION

**The BADASS chooses to take the burden off his customers' plate.**

The BADASS knows that there is strength in simplicity and ease. Customers are looking to you to simplify their lives and make purchasing your product or service easier.

When I owned and operated Rainmakers Marketing Group Inc., the Sales Agency representing American Standard brands, we created a simple "cheat sheet" that had the top product selections for the commercial and residential channels. All the global manufacturers in the plumbing industry had massive catalogues filled with a huge range of products. Often, these books would be inches thick. The American Standard price books were binder size and two inches wide, with the specification guides four to five inches thick. When we called on engineers, designers, architects, and builders many of them found the books overwhelming and difficult to navigate. The same could be said about some websites.

Differentiating the onslaught of products was a nightmare for our customers. I realized that they were overwhelmed with the product offering, and often made mistakes when specifying products. This meant a lot of follow up work to resolve the issues and proved frustrating for everyone.

**TIP: Focus on selling products and services that are easy to sell and trouble free.**

In an effort to differentiate and simplify the process for clients, I decided to create "cheat sheets" with the most popular items and their corresponding products, presenting them in a package or bundled format. I chose the top three selling products for each category, presenting them as best-better-good approach with dollar sign symbols ($ - $$$) to quickly identify where the product sat on the price continuum.

**TIP: Make everything as easy as possible for customers and they will buy from you.**

The sheets also included a photo of the product, individual product specifications in short bullet form format and a quick write-up detailing the benefits of using the product. I was able to take the manufacturer's giant book and downsize it to two pages of the most popular and top-selling items, making it easy to use.

**TIP: You should always present your most expensive product first, and always in groups of threes. When given a choice, most people select one. If you present the expensive one first, most are likely to choose the mid-priced option over the entry level one.**

***"Present in threes and the customer is likely to say 'Yes, please.'"***

—Jackie Rainforth

Customers could pull out the sheets and quickly choose the product fixtures they wanted with ease. We also presented them in packages or bundles (faucet, sink, toilet and urinal), often resulting in us selling our Manufacturer as the choice of brand for all their selections, securing the specification and making a larger sale at the same time.

Customer efficiency improved because they were not wasting time flipping through pages or making costly mistakes. They had a price ladder reference which simplified the process for them making it easy to buy according to price point. Their product knowledge and familiarity with the line substantially improved allowing them to actively promote our products with their customers.

We made the purchasing procedure so simple, that they supported us fully. Not only did our brand gain noteworthy momentum and market share (it went from the bottom of the heap to #1 in Alberta), it brought in some healthy commissions. We clearly distinguished our process from our competitors, allowing us to markedly outperform them. This proved to exponentially improve the number of specifications we received, which meant greater revenues, fewer specification changes and higher sales. Selling a higher quality product meant increased profit margins. Better quality products resulted in fewer service calls or maintenance issues, and it streamlined the inventory.

**TIP: Always focus on higher-margin products to maximize profitability. Profitability always trumps sales.**

By selling a larger quantity of the same items, more frequently, we improved inventory supply and turns, which lead to increased profitability. The product spent less time on the shelves, enhanced the internal purchasing process, and allowed for better product availability and delivery for our customers.

**TIP: Always look for ways to streamline your inventory by maximizing sales of one product or service. Do so through focus and promotion of that item.**

It was a win/win for all. What turned out to be a tool to simplify the lives of our customers, paid with huge financial dividends for us.

## NICHE DIFFERENTIATION

**The BADASS looks and thrives on the gaps his competitors miss.**

Look for areas in your industry to create niche markets, which in turn can create phenomenal brand loyalty. I have used this concept to my advantage throughout my career.

When selling plumbing fixtures for construction, I quickly realized that the manufacturers salespeople were only calling on the distributors and the contractors—leaving the product selection process vulnerable to product substitution. No one was calling on the specifiers or the true decision makers; architects, designers and engineers. They would work directly with the building owners, as they designed the buildings from concept to creation. These groups were the ones in fact who decided on the products that would be used in all the construction projects. An out of the box thinker, I set up sales teams to specifically call on these influencers. By calling on the decision makers versus leaving the choice of product to be influenced by contractors and distributors, we gained a higher degree of control over the products selected and left less room for substitution or change by others, who may have lacked brand loyalty to our product line.

**TIPS:**

- **Always look for the decision maker when selling.**
- **Always think outside of the box, finding ways to do things differently. The goal is to stand out and be positively noticed for being unique and different.**

Our business exploded.

**TIP: First to market becomes and stays top of mind.**

## EXCLUSIVITY DIFFERENTIATION

**The BADASS SUPERSTAR creates creative programs.**

When niche differentiation is not available, create it through exclusivity and tiered agreement offerings. You are better off to limit the number of people you sell to, increasing their loyalty and dedication, rather than trying to be everything to everybody.

Kohler, the luxury plumbing manufacturer made a bold but lucrative decision to limit their product line distribution to only one or two distributors. This allowed rival manufacturers to deal with the remaining suppliers. It was a win/win as they created aligned partnerships, increasing revenues for all.

They then took their exclusivity one step further. They offered limited tiered distribution levels to clients. Allowing only one Premiere showroom per province, the recipient would get exclusive offerings, price advantages with minimum purchasing agreements, no-cost sampling and additional benefits and services. Standard showrooms received basic services, pricing and sampling. It was a get-what-you-pay-for agreement allowing Kohler to spend more time and money on the customers who supported them the most. The more you paid, and the more you supported the line, the more advantages you received. Kohler ultimately created their own niche market, resulting in increased loyalty and product alignment.

**TIP: Exclusivity = Profitability.**

Look for opportunities in your industry to make the most of exclusive and (or) tiered agreements, allowing you to create your own niche markets.

## SERVICE DIFFERENTIATION

**BADASS SUPERSTARS work to create the ultimate customer experience.**

The BADASS knows there is no bigger value proposition than providing unbeatable customer service. It is one of the most common and effective ways used to differentiate from competitors.

At I-XL BUILDING PRODUCTS Ltd., I quickly determined that new home buyers were left to their own devices when making their exterior brick color selections. With approval from my superiors, I took photos of homes showcasing all our various brick and stone colors and sourced samples from all of the other exterior suppliers including stucco, siding, soffit, fascia, roof and windows. Then I had showroom referral cards made up, complete with our contact information, a map to get to our location and personally went to show homes and spoke to the assigned realtor or builder personnel. We advertised that if they sent their new home purchasers our way, we would assist the homeowners with their complete exterior selections. We provided a design service, ensuring their colors coordinated, with the added advantage of one stop shopping. Instead of having to go to five different exterior companies, and not remember what color they picked where, we would help them do it all, faster with cohesive results.

**TIP: Service is the easiest way to differentiate.**

Did I get pushback from some within the company when I suggested it? You bet! They felt I was promoting the competition. I had taken the time to understand the market and customer needs and knew that builders and homeowners would not financially support an entire house completely "wrapped" in brick or stone (the sales focus at the time). What they did want was a smaller amount of brick and stone to add depth and customization to their home. They also wanted the simplicity of a selection process, with the assurance that their color choices would match. A home is likely the single largest financial investment people make. They wanted to make sure it would look good, maximizing their curb appeal and return on investment.

**TIP: Always look for ways to do the added extras for your customer.**

People loved our new service offering! They were confident in their choices and it led to a higher number of clients putting our products on their new homes. The added bonus; product per home was used as we were able to suggest and influence their purchasing decision as experts in the field. Our creative approach blew our competitors out of the water, catapulting our sales and cementing our brand in the marketplace!

**TIP: Collaborating or joint venturing with others in creative ways can bring surprising benefits.**

Shelley Stelfox, an entrepreneurial superstar, life-long friend and founder of Old Smokey Meats in Fresno California shares this:

> ***"Selling is like fashion. It is about staying ahead of your customer the way a designer stays abreast of the trends. Things are always changing. If you become stagnant, people will lose interest. You must always keep things easy and interesting for them."***

The BADASS SUPERSTAR knows one of the best ways to gain a substantive advantage is by looking at the bigger picture to seek innovation within your industry and find ways to differentiate. What can you bring to the market that is currently missing, knowing that customers will pay a higher price for?

Actively look for gaps and innovative solutions only you can provide. Make every product and process the best in its space and then market those strengths and weaknesses over your competitors. Seek uniqueness, individuality and excellence in all that you do.

**TIP: Stay focused on your own game instead of trying to match others because a BADASS SUPERSTAR forges their own path.**

# CHAPTER 7

# *Prepare, Prepare,* PREPARE

**A BADASS is always mentally, physically and strategically prepared.**

The better prepared you are, the more confident and professional you will be. BADASS SUPERSTARS know what to do, how to do it, and create a strategic plan they can consistently rely on, setting themselves up to maximize their opportunities. By having processes in place, that they can mentally follow, they can exponentially improve their overall success rate.

It is surprising to see how many people in sales do not take the time to prepare, and simply 'wing it'. In fact, 50% have no idea what questions they are going to ask when they walk into a meeting. As Kieran Longworth, Partner and Sales Expert from the renowned recruiting firm, Lock Search Group puts it so well:

***"Preparation is massive! You can't just roll in on personality and flash!"***

The left side of our brain gives us our analytic, logic, thinking, sequencing and reasoning capabilities. The right side, our creative, emotional, intuition, visualization and multitasking side. Being prepared gives you confidence. Confidence keeps you in the left side of the brain. Lose your confidence and you will automatically switch to the emotional, less organized side leading to lost sales, missed opportunities, giving away bigger discounts than intended, or being perceived as unprofessional.

Yes, extra work and effort are required, however, more often than not, taking the time to be prepared secures one's confidence and ability to quickly flex and adjust to today's unpredictable and growingly complicated sales process.

## BE ENTHUSIASTIC AND ENERGENTIC

**A BADASS knows energy and enthusiasm are contagious.**

Enthusiasm is the most important personal factor in selling. It is the transfer of an emotional commitment. It is important to have high energy when seeing a client. Yes, you should be mirroring them in terms of their level of energy. However, being positive and passionate are critical. People need to know you love your product and love what you are doing—that you are excited to be there—before they will get on board and buy in. Your energy and enthusiasm will prompt them to join in the experience.

> **TIP: Do a BADASS SUPERMAN POWER POSE to reinvigorate your energy level before you make a call. With feet spread apart, back straight, head tall, take a deep breath punch both hands up in the air with energy and enthusiasm and say YEAH!**

## PARK THE EGO

**The BADASS SUPERSTAR does not let success get to their head.**

Humility in salespeople is crucial and more important today than ever with our distrusting society. People need to know you, like you and trust you. Being humble is a part of that. As salespeople we have to have confidence, faith and belief in ourselves, but overinflated or exaggerated confidence can become ego, which is about self-interest. Humility on the other hand, is a modest view of one's own self-importance. It shows others that you place yourself at the same level as others and is a skill of self-control which is perceived to be the real measure of leadership and success.

Offensive ego shows up in the need to be acknowledged, heard, and respected while defensive ego stems from protecting yourself from failure, being hurt and being judged.

Defensive ego is the destructive ego that feeds aggressive and unhealthy competition. Ask yourself, "Do I feel better than others?" "Do I feel inferior to others?" If you answered yes to either of these, you might see the signs of unhealthy ego:

- The I am right – you are wrong mentality. Is it better to be happy, or to be right? Because there certainly are costs involved.
- The win at all costs attitude. You will do and say whatever it takes to win. This is where integrity comes into play. You would rather win than do your best.
- Unwillingness to back down in a conversation or argument.
- Constant comparison showing jealousy towards others who are happier, better looking, more intelligent or wealthier. Or the opposite, those who are less than.
- Blaming others and making excuses instead of taking responsibility.
- Gossiping about others.
- Sulking instead of feeling pride for doing a job well done when defeated.
- Setting impossible goals and berating yourself when you fall short.

Watch for these. Unfortunately, they can highjack your business and destroy the good you have worked so hard to achieve. When it comes to this topic, Kieran Longworth, Sales Specialist from Lock Search Group of Recruiters states:

***"Salespeople naturally have a swagger and ego. Being humble is critical in today's culture. People want to deal with others who are 'real'."***

Bruce Cruikshank, Founder and Business Performance Management Specialist from EK Communications who specializes in helping businesses with strategy, culture and process follows that with:

***"When people let sales success go to their head, they get a big ego and they feel they know better. They start telling the customer instead of asking, listening and trusting the process."***

Do not let an overactive ego tap your potential to be the BADASS SUPERSTAR you know you can be. Set a standard of excellence for yourself. I once let my ego get the best of me. Big mistake. It was the unhappiest time of my life.

## NO GOALS, NO GROWTH

**BADASS SUPERSTARS set goals to maintain focus and accountability.**

They have clearly defined priorities which eliminates distraction and helps them stay on course. We all know we should write our goals down, but sadly, only 20% of us do. In fact, too often, we become lazy and make the excuse that we have our goals in our head.

Harvard Business School did a study on their students who defined their career and financial aspirations after graduating. There were three groups:

- **Group #1:** 84% had no goals.
- **Group #2:** 13% had goals in their minds but did not write them down.
- **Group #3:** 3% had written goals and plans to accomplish them.

After 10 years, the results were as follows:

- The 13% who had goals, but **DID NOT** write them down, **EARNED TWICE** the amount of those who had no goals at all.
- The 3% who DID write them down, **EARNED TEN TIMES** as much as the other 97% of groups combined.

Setting goals and creating a plan can dramatically increase your results. Writing down why they are important and visualizing how you are going to reap the reward is equally significant.

I visited the top-selling New Home Salesperson for a Home Builder client I was working with. I interview all staff member before doing a series of sales training to let them know I am there to support them and help them meet their individual goals. We were discussing goal setting when she pulled out her book out and opened it up. I was completely blown away. There in black and white, neatly written, were all her goals for the day. With a flip of the pages, she had her weekly, monthly, and yearly goals complete with comments, checkmarks and X's indicating "accomplished", at her fingertips for regular review. No wonder she is a top earning Superstar at her company! She uses her goals to stay focused and on track, understanding that each one is a step towards earning the income she wants.

The key to accomplishing your goals is to break them down into smaller achievable tasks, be diligent in following through, and record your progress. Reviewing your goals can inspire and motivate, especially on those low energy days when you need that extra boost.

***"If you can improve your performance just one per cent each day in any facet of your life, you'll be one and a half times as good at it in 41 days and twice as good in just 70 days."***

—Selling Power

**TIP: Writing journal entries is another way to successfully create personal accountability. At the end of each day I write down all the things I have done to promote or move my business forward. It is a great way to keep focused on my business.**

## CONTINUAL LEARNING

**A BADASS knows that to stop learning is to stop growing.**

Personal development is the building block for extending your influence and reach. Continual and active learning over a lifetime, is a common thread amongst the BADASS. Empowering yourself with knowledge, staying on top of the emerging trends, shifts or changes in your industry is a Superstar necessity because we know that change is continuous and inevitable.

Shane Wenzel, an industry inspiration and President of the Shane Homes Group of Companies shares his perspective:

***"I see a lot of salespeople fail because they think they know it all. They stop learning. Once you are done with learning, you are on a downward slope. You need to stay current with the times because the market is always changing."***

Continual learning is an essential part of succeeding in today's era. Working hard to become a knowledgeable and informed value-add partner, makes us a priceless resource to our clients. It is about becoming the industry, not just existing in it. Superstars know that our world is changing at accelerated rates, and in order to maintain a competitive advantage, being informed and knowledgeable gives us an edge over the competition.

A SUPERSTAR always does more. They make the time to stay current by reading books, blogs, and articles, as well as listen to podcasts and participate in webinars. Subscribing to magazines, following experts online or joining sales groups makes learning easy. For those who are really serious about their knowledge and performance, taking courses, joining a mindset group, having a coach or regularly attending industry association meetings, can also be great sources of information. But watch out, as we can also become easily distracted. Assign a specific amount of time to these activities and stick to it. Balance and moderation are vital.

***"The average person spends 50 minutes a day on Facebook, Instagram and Messenger."***

—Mark Zuckerberg

**TIP: The iPhone has a setting that monitors and breaks down your usage. Open SETTINGS, go to BATTERY USAGE, and tap on the little CLOCK icon. You may be surprised at how much time you spend online.**

Selling today is about becoming the industry, not just existing in it. Superstars know that our world is changing at accelerated rates and in order to maintain a competitive advantage, being informed, knowledgeable and networked is essential. Knowing everything we can about what is going on in our industry, gives us a favorable and esteemed position with customers.

## FINANCIAL ANALYSIS

**A BADASS understands that knowing your numbers is essential in making good decisions.**

If you take over an existing client list, do a thorough review of the sales reports and compare numbers. Look for patterns and trends. Know your numbers, financial strengths and weaknesses, what products are doing well, and which ones are not. Understand where the sales are coming from, why you are successful and where you are falling short.

- Who are the top 1% and 5% customers?
- What are the top product categories?
- Who are the A-Best group of customers? You are their #1 supplier. Find out why.
- Who are the B-Top 25% of customers? You provide most of their product. Are their expectations continuing to be met?
- Who are the C-Mid 25% of the customer? They purchase very little – is there an opportunity for growth?
- And finally, who are the D-Lowest 25? They buy very little - find out why.

Identify the specific areas where you think there is room to grow, with whom, with what products, and how you think you can achieve that growth. Create lists and remember to go after the most viable first.

## VEHICLE KIT

**The BADASS SUPERSTAR knows good organization leads to time saved.**

Before you start making sales calls, be sure to have back up presentation materials in your vehicle. This type of preparedness eliminates the wasted time having to schedule additional meetings, while giving the ability to close the sale immediately. It is an efficiency that saves time, money and achieves faster results. Prepare the items so they are organized and easily accessible to you in your car; literature, samples, order forms, cheat sheets, extra pens, paper, business cards etc. and restock it regularly.

### TIPS:

- **A BADASS SUPERSTAR is NEVER without a pen, paper, his schedule, phone or business cards.**
- **Women should only ever carry one bag into a sales presentation. Carrying more than one or having her hands full can lead others to assume she is disorganized.**

## THE CONVERSATION BLUEPRINT

**The BADASS knows preparation is time well spent.**

Preparing a conversation blueprint in writing helps to mentally guide you through the sales process. These days, meetings can take various turns and deviations from the expected conversation. Write out in point form the important concepts, statements or questions you want to include and discuss. This is only an outline of the conversation, that you would like to follow.

As Bruce Cruikshank suggests:

> ***"What are the step-by-step events that will take place in the meeting? Map it out and apply it consistently. Evaluate what is or is not working, so you can adjust and manage it every day."***

**TIP: I always jot down a few key words prior to meeting with a client or making a call. It keeps me on track when the conversation goes off in a different direction, reminding me of the points I want to discuss.**

# CHAPTER 8

# *Badass Selling—the* PRESENTATION

**A BADASS knows the goal in selling is to be a solution provider to their customers.**

Although referred to as a presentation, I consider it a well-planned, mapped out conversation. Salespeople need to be thinking on their feet, anticipating and strategizing all the time. Be well prepared, with an outline and have specific value-add points that you would like to target during the conversation. The more natural and genuine you can make your time with your prospect or client feel, the more successful your results will be. No one likes being sold, so stay away from the scripted selling. Make it more like a conversation between friends, and your sales results will have more depth and connectedness.

## BUILD REAL RAPPORT

**A BADASS is an expert at building relationships.**

Before you start talking business, it is important to build rapport with your prospect. Discover outside interests, like sports, hobbies and children. Have they been in the news lately? Received an award? Did a mutual connection put you in touch? Were you interacting online? With time being such a valuable commodity these days, it is always better to start off with business topics. Finding commonalities of any type will help to build a stronger bond and get the conversation off to a good start.

At the same time, look around their office, watch their mannerisms, body language and identify their personality type which will give you clues to their purchasing triggers. Be curious and authentic in taking an interest. People can tell when you're faking it. Be genuinely empathetic, demonstrating you can see their point of view.

When people are comfortable with you, they are more open to your suggestions, are willing to hear the solutions you offer, with greater acceptance.

> ***"Trust is rated as the #1 most influential factor when closing a deal ranking higher than price or return on investment."***
>
> —LinkedIn

Buyers want personalization from sellers and want to buy from people who are like them. Identifying commonalities can make a big difference in the quality and pace of the relationship. Start off by having a low key, friendly dialog. As mentioned, people like to say yes to those they like. When conversing, mirror their energy level.

> **TIP: Speaking the person's name is the biggest compliment you can give them.**

The biggest mistake salespeople make when building rapport is they try to be too friendly too soon or they stay in the surface stage of conversation for far too long, boring the prospect. They come across as phony or lacking in sincerity, or worse, seen as having a lack of respect for time and business. Instead, be curious and interested in their thoughts, feelings and opinions and then casually lead into the matter of business. Your focus should be on asking questions, with a genuine interest in the person.

As Dale Carnegie suggests in the book *WINNING FRIENDS & INFLUENCING PEOPLE*, the best way to get people to bond and connect is by getting them to talk about themselves.

**TIP: Every salesperson should read Dale Carnegie's book. I have gone back to it numerous times throughout my career. It is a wonderful reminder.**

Rapport does not necessarily have to happen in a formal location such as their office. It can be done anywhere and can happen at any time. Furthermore, creating new business does not necessarily have to be the intent:

This is exactly what happened when I attended a seminar. A number of attendees, unknown to each other, gathered during the break for lunch. Sitting at a table we were having a casual conversation getting to know one another, sharing stories, asking questions. It was a wonderful dialog. The next day, I was completely taken aback and wonderfully surprised when one of the attendees, a business owner, asked me to provide training for her company. I was astonished and greatly appreciative!

Never underestimate the power of rapport.

If a relationship has not been established, it becomes difficult and awkward, making it highly unlikely the deal will close. Remember, they need to know you, like you and trust you before they will buy. Organizations seek salespeople who reliably excel in their ability to quickly create alliances and build strong relationships with customers. It all starts with building rapport.

# TAKE NOTES

**A BADASS pays attention to the smallest of details.**

Do not make the mistake of thinking you can rely on your memory to remind you of what is important to your client, the commitments you have made, or the requests they asked for. When you are meeting with or speaking to a customer, it is imperative to take notes. Yes, we are in a technological age and we have many ways to record. If you are going to take notes on a smart device, it is imperative that you let your client know. Do not let them make assumptions.

I had this happen once. I had a new, younger employee with me who started tapping away on her cell phone during the meeting with a client. You could see the customer was getting very annoyed, as it looked like the employee was totally immersed and preoccupied with other more pressing matters than the conversation at hand. The perception was that she was extremely rude. She did not tell me until afterwards that she was, in fact, taking detailed notes about the conversation. Although she later phoned and explained her actions to the customer, unfortunately, first impressions last.

Handwritten notes are still preferred, and have many advantages:

- Your ability to make eye contact throughout the interaction is better than using a device.
- The person you are with will feel valued because what they are saying, and their contribution will be deemed as important.
- It shows that you are actively listening to your client.
- It shows the client that you have the intention of following up.

- You can record your own thoughts and reminders at the same time.
- It gives you the ability to make a note of keywords that will act as a reminder to bring up topics later in the conversation or ask more questions as the conversation moves forward.
- It allows you to write down their objections so you can specifically address later in the conversation.

**TIP: If you ask for permission to take notes, most people will be more thoughtful with their answers, often giving more elaborate information, which is always an added benefit.**

Remembering every point discussed in a conversation is an impossible feat, where even the major concepts get fuzzy over time. Once you have the notes, they become an invaluable tool. A detailed record and a reminder of the commitments you made, the requests your client asked for and the follow-up work that must be done. They can be used as a guideline of the important points discussed when sending a 're-cap' back to your client or as the foundation when you create an account strategy moving forward.

As your relationship with a client progresses, you will not have the opportunity to go back and ask the initial discovery questions again. Notes become helpful in recalling those conversations, giving you the opportunity to review and refresh your mind at a later point in time. There have been many times where I have often referred back to my notes for clarification.

***"Those who take notes are able to recall about 23% more nuggets of information than people who didn't take notes."***

—Leadership IQ

It still surprises me at how few salespeople take notes. Taking effective notes is an essential skillset of selling that will serve you well on so many levels, but it also projects an image of professionalism in the eyes of the client.

## INSIGHTFUL AND PROVOCATIVE QUESTIONS

**The BADASS knows that the quality of the questions asked determines the quality of the outcome.**

Asking good questions and a lot of them is the key to becoming a BADASS Superstar! The more insightful the questions, the more detailed and valuable the information you will receive. The goal is to discover the emotional need behind their pain points or challenges, what keeps them up at night, what causes them stress and the source of friction that needs to be resolved. Become a discovery expert.

### Common Discovery Mistakes

There are three common mistakes that I see salespeople make all the time when it comes to asking questions:

- **Fail to Listen:** Instead of listening, they dive right into their presentation. Remember, it isn't about how much product knowledge you have, it is about solving their problem and finding an effective solution that works for the client.

- **Make Assumptions:** Some salespeople think they know what the customer wants and needs, altogether neglecting to ask questions. They start discussing why they are, their company and their product is the best without regard for what the customer feels is important.

- **Blah Blah Blah Questions:** The everyday, surface-type questions that don't inspire, motivate or engage the client should be completely avoided. They limit the information and feedback received. Instead they choose to ask questions that require thought and consideration when answering. Remember: garbage in, garbage out.

Today, our attention spans are shorter than ever. Jeff Shore compares it to a stop light. You only have a limited time before you lose the customer's attention, and the light quickly turns to yellow, then red, ending your conversation.

Take the time to write and memorize a variety of thought-provoking discovery questions specific to your client and to explore the issues to uncover the motivational needs. I love questions that ask in threes because they maximize your opportunities and the quality of the information you receive back. Questions in threes will bring the most value from their answers.

## Questions to Delve in and Discover

There are a variety of ways you can ask questions to help you establish the core needs of a client:

- **Ask 10 Questions in a Row:** All salespeople love to talk, but a good reminder to stay focused on delving deeper is to make a habit of asking ten questions in a row. This is particularly important for people new to sales. Making this a habit will help you identify what is driving your customer in their purchasing decision.

- **Ask for Three Examples:** Asking for three examples affords you the opportunity to solve up to three challenges and provide multiple solutions. It will help you in better improving your odds of creating a wow experience for the customer. Also, it shows them that you are highly strategic and are willing to tackle multiple tasks.

  Ask questions such as:

  - "What are the top three biggest challenges?"
  - "What key outcomes do you want?"
  - "What three benefits would you achieve if those challenges were resolved?"

- **Past/Present/Future:** Knowing the events leading up to the presentation can provide an invaluable understanding of the circumstances.

  - Past – "What has happened in the past that brought you to this point?"
  - Present – "What is happening now and what are you currently looking for?"
  - Future – "What results would you like to see in the future?"

- **Delve Deeper x Three:** When a prospect answers one question, ask three more questions, each one digging a little deeper to provide more clarification.

- **Ask Multiple Choice Questions:** Give your client a choice or an option and it will almost always result in a selection.

When you ask questions, start with the most general questions first and narrow down to the more specific. Who/What/Where/When are ideal lead-ins for asking questions: Why is a good one to use when gaining clarification and deepens understanding. You need to know the problems, goals and preferences of your clients to serve them well.

## LISTEN, LISTEN, LISTEN

**The BADASS knows that 70% of the conversation should be spent listening.**

Active listening is probably the one area where most salespeople fail miserably. Everyone loves to talk, and salespeople are no exception. They are more concerned about doing their presentation than listening to what the customer is saying. Or they are busy thinking about what they are going to say next instead of being attuned to what the customer is really saying. When a customer speaks, listen not only to what he is saying but how they are saying it and look for any innuendo behind the comments. Listening well allows you to interpret their attitude and mood.

As professional salespeople, you often need to use your intuition and read between the lines. You cannot do that when you are busy planning your pitch. That is why it is important to be prepared.

SUPERSTARS listen intently, uncovering all that is being communicated. Be sure to show communication agreement signs… Nod, Uhmm, Yes, I see… and to paraphrase what they said to confirm you are on the same track "So what you are saying is…" Doing so shows the prospect you are engaged and actively listening.

## AVOID THE PRODUCT DUMP

**The BADASS SUPERSTAR knows that you don't sell the same to everyone.**

Too often, salespeople will do a PRODUCT DUMP. They go through every feature and benefit, rifling through their presentation hoping something sticks. As Rose-Ann Normandeau, founder of the chain of Normandeau Window Coverings, who holds the coveted Centurion Gallery title from Hunter Douglas revealed:

***"I cannot tell you how many times a week someone tries to sell to me in that exact format—they come in and say, 'I am great, my product is great, this is what it does, and you are going to love it!' Not one question is asked. They have no idea if I even need it! It is beyond annoying!"***

# CHAPTER 9

# *Meet Needs to* SUCCEED

**We cannot sell if 100% of our focus is not on meeting the needs of the clients.**

This is where you put yourself in the shoes of the customer. What are the reasons and motivation behind their reason to buy? And how do I make sure every comment I make from this point onward is about meeting their needs?

## SOLUTION RESOLUTION

**BADASS SUPERSTARS bring solutions and value.**

Selling is about providing a solution or gain that resolves the customer's challenge or issue, by presenting as value-add solutions.

Buy-in must follow a sequential order. A salesperson must sell themselves, then the company and finally the product, maintaining this order. If it is done out of sequence, you will likely not move forward in the process.

For example, if you try to sell the product first, and have not built credibility or rapport with the client, chances are they are not going to buy. They need to like you and trust you first. This rule of thumb becomes irrelevant when selling a commodity product.

If they like you and like your product, but have not bought into the company, the process will be blocked.

## THE REAL REASON

**A BADASS knows that people buy on emotion and justify with logic.**

The emotional need is the payoff the customer will receive as a result of buying your product or service. There are six basic emotions that evoke one to buy:

- **Greed:** "If I make a decision now, I will be rewarded, or it will pay off later."
- **Fear:** "If I don't make this decision now, it will result in a negative consequence."
- **Altruism:** *"If I make this decision, it will benefit others."*
- **Envy:** *"If I make this decision now, I will beat/outperform my competition."*
- **Pride:** *"If I make this decision, I will look good/smart."*
- **Shame:** *"If I don't make this decision now, I will avoid looking stupid/incompetent."*

Identifying the underlying emotion behind the purchasing decision has been one of my biggest tickets to success.

## DEEPER EMOTIONAL NEED

**A BADASS knows finding the emotional connection makes it easier to close the sale.**

The deeper need is typically a larger goal that the decision maker wants to accomplish, and it is emotionally driven. If you can determine the emotional driver behind the decision-making process and key in on it, you will multiply your sales beyond your wildest dreams.

Below is an example of how you can Delve Deeper x THREE questions. Going from general to specific can help you identify the lead's emotional need. Do not stop asking questions until you hit the emotion driving the decision:

**General:** **"Can you tell me a little more about why you are looking at this <Product>?"**

*Answer:* ***"I want our business to run more effectively."***

**Ask #1:** **"What 3 specific things would you want to run more effectively?"**

*Answer:* ***"I would like our team to spend less time doing <1, 2, and 3>."***

**Ask #2:** **"Is there anything else you would like it to do?"**

*Answer:* ***"Yes I would like to save money and improve efficiency."***

**Ask #3:** **"And is there a particular reason why being more efficient, spending less time <1, 2, and 3>", and finding cost savings are important to you right now?**

*Answer:* ***"Yes, I want to maximize the Company's resale value, so I can retire comfortably."***

"Retiring comfortably" is the emotional driver that will prompt him to move forward. If you can resolve his three efficiency issues and present your specific features and benefits in a way that reinforces his true need—the ability to retire—you will be able to close the sale. Always probe until you have a clear picture of what they are trying to accomplish or improve.

## My Two Secret Words

BADASS SUPERSTARS consistently link the feature (what it is), the benefit (what it does) and the emotional need together when presenting. The secret to do so is in my two secret words: which means. Each feature and benefit presented should further drive the emotional need:

**FEATURE: What it is.**

*"This <product or service> has <5 Speed Cycles>."*

**BENEFIT: What it does.**

*"That enables it to <improve efficiency>."*

**EMOTIONAL NEED:**

*"which means you can increase the re-sale value of the company and retire comfortably."*

Your ability to persuade others by appealing to their deeper emotional needs will have a dramatic effect on your sales. The more you can elicit positive emotions, and drive emotional resolution when selling to someone, the closer that client will feel towards you. The closer they feel, the more they buy.

## Know the Needs

All customers are looking for you to answer the following:

- Why should I listen to you? Sell Yourself.
- What does it do? Why is it special? Sell the Features.
- How is it going to improve my life? Sell the Benefits.
- Who else has bought it? Looking for testimonials.
- Who says it is good? Looking for word of mouth.
- How does it meet my needs? Meet the deeper need.
- Why it is the right choice? What exactly do I get? The Big Benefit.

# CHAPTER 10

# *Wrapping* IT UP

**Overcoming Objections and asking for the close are essential skills in selling.**

But if you have asked the right questions, discovered the motivators and presented the right features and benefits to meet the deeper need, the final stages of the selling process become simple and straightforward.

## TEST THE TEMPERATURE

**A BADASS knows to close throughout the presentation—success leaves clues.**

Trial Closing is about taking the person's temperature throughout the process to ensure you are on the right track. As you present each feature/benefit/emotional link, check in and test the readiness of the buyer, checking the customer's reaction. Move ahead ONLY when you know that your explanation was relevant, and that the customer has accepted the benefits you have described.

### After each selling point, check their reaction:

- "Does that work for you?"
- "Any concerns so far?"
- "Are we good to continue?"

If they respond favourably, close the sale. If they have a negative response (an objection) you have work to do before you can move to the next step. By taking their temperature along the way, the customer's answers will guide you, letting you know what you need to do. If you handle this part of the presentation well, the close becomes a simple statement.

## EASILY OVERCOME OBJECTIONS

**A BADASS expects the YES and embraces hearing the NO.**

An objection is actually a very good thing, yet most people fear the pushback. As a culture, the natural reaction and response to salespeople is to say NO. If you get an objection, this means your customer is still interested, but you have not convinced them that your product or service is right for them.

**STEP 1: ACKNOWLEDGE the objection.**

- "I see."
- "I understand."

**STEP 2: DELVE DEEPER by asking another question, clarifying the objection.**

- "Why do you feel that way?"
- "Can you please explain?"
- "What are you comparing it too?"

**STEP 3: PROVE VALUE to diffuse the objection. Areas of value:**

- Improved Efficiency
- Saved Time

- Saved Money
- Creation of Money
- Return on Investment (ROI is the #1 value Salespeople should prove and focus on)

**STEP 4: GET PERMISSION to move forward.**

- Know what the common objections are and practice overcoming them so you can handle seamlessly. **ALWAYS RESPOND TO AN OBJECTION—NEVER IGNORE IT.**

Handling objections is an essential skill in selling. Many people are weak in this area and as a result, their emotional fight or flight response is triggered. That can be easily avoided by being prepared. You must be confident. Recognize that old feeling of fear and push through.

## CONFIDENT CLOSING

**The BADASS knows that obstacles are the stepping stones to success.**

Closing is the final stage. Too often, salespeople clam up when it comes to asking that one final question. Fear overtakes them. They completely neglect to ask for the order, often losing the losing the sale. Don't let this happen to you.

I went to a Home and Garden convention a few years ago. I was looking at a fairly expensive garden awning product. The salesman asked me a lot of great questions discovering my wants and needs. Then he went through all the features and benefits that were specific to what I was looking for. He did an incredible job.

I was ready to buy!

But instead, we just stood there in uncomfortable silence. I was waiting for him to ask me for the order, to close the sale, but he never did. Awkwardly, he turned away. I just stood there for a minute and then exited from the booth. I bought from a competitor.

Push through the fear! What is the worst that can happen? They say NO?!

Closing, like handling objections, needs practice, practice and more practice. That is why my program is so full of role-play. Practice at home with you partner, with a friend, with the dog.

## Closing Questions:

- "Would you like this option or that option?"
- "How would you like to pay?"
- "Do you want to go ahead and give it a try?"
- "How would you like to move forward?"
- "When would you like it delivered?"
- "Does what I am offering solve your problem?"

**NOTE: ALWAYS ASKING FOR THE CLOSE** is one of the biggest challenges some salespeople have. Again, this is where we circle back to the fear that holds us back.

***"Forty-eight per cent of sales calls end with the salesperson failing to ask for the close."***

—Brian Tracy

Uri Hess, CEO of Hess L& D Inc., and mentor to many, gives us some great advice with:

***"It's a fear of rejection. Too many salespeople want the customer to close for them, however, the successful salesperson always asks for the order. The customer may be sceptical, nervous, or may want you to work harder for the sale, but until they have clearly rejected the proposal, recognize that they haven't said no."***

Closing should not invoke fear and insecurity but provide a harmonious end to the sales cycle and a job well done. If you follow the simple steps to prepare well, and check for assurance along the way, closing becomes easy. Like anything, the more we do it, the better we become.

## NOW OR NEVER

**THE BADASS knows to close it or they will lose it!**

The best time to close a deal is now! If the prospect leaves, chances are you will never have a second opportunity. People buy on emotional impulse, that is why it is important to ask for the close while the emotion is high.

**TIP: The longer people have engaged in, or negotiated on a product or service, the more invested and devoted they will become towards finalizing the deal.**

We also know that today's customer and the purchasing process takes multiple visits. It is for that reason that one should always book the next appointment before the conversation ends. Just like the buyer who walks away is less likely to come back and make the purchase, if you leave without booking another appointment, your opportunity to do so after the fact, substantially deteriorates.

# CHAPTER 11

# *Fierce* FOLLOW UP

**The BADASS knows fierce follow up is the difference between the adequate and the extraordinary.**

We see it over and over, salespeople who fail to follow up. The key is to create systems. If you are a Sales Professional, do some quick self-analysis and ask yourself:

- "Have I been following up with my customers?"
- "Have I done everything they asked me to do?"
- "Have I done what I said I would?"

Unfortunately, the answer is often NO. This tends to be one of the biggest complaints, causing frustrated and angry clients. It is one of the principal reasons why some salespeople never see the success they desire.

It is the seemingly non-important "little stuff" that often matters the most.

- Did you email the information the Customer asked for?
- Did you deliver the literature you promised?
- Did you call the Customer back when you said you would?
- Did you take care of that annoying invoice error that they asked to have taken care of?
- Are you following through on ALL commitments made?

Yes, this seems so easy, yet so many people fail to do it.

The average person forgets 50%–75% of any conversation by the day's end. Think about it. How many sales calls do you make in a day? How much are you forgetting by the end of the week? It is impossible to remember everything unless you keep notes and even then, it requires a system. Too often, salespeople fail to follow up, not on purpose, but because they have neglected to put a process in place. Systems create habits and habits become the fail-safes for highly effective people.

## PROCESS IS PROVEN

**A BADASS is an expert in tying up the loose ends.**

Implementing consistent systems to ensure you follow through on commitments will probably do more for your career than anything else. It is crucial to create processes to make sure you are taking care of your clients' requests and wishes. Make it a habit and it will serve you well.

### Write to Ignite Follow Up

Take detailed hand-written notes and stay organized. I use a Daytimer; pre-dated, two pages per day. You can buy extra pages and all sorts of helpful accessories. Mobile Apps and CRM can do the same thing for you. Set aside regular time at the end of the day/week to go through your notes from each meeting.

- Ensure the customer name and date are noted at the top of the page. I know it sounds like a no-brainer, but I cannot tell you how many times I have missed it, which leaves me fumbling and wasting a ton of time.

- Mark any commitments you make, or customer requests with a big asterisk. Preferably do this during the meeting, making it quick and easy to spot during follow up.
- Go through your tasks. Once completed, highlight the items in your notes to confirm that it is done and then move onto the next.
- When you have completed all, file the paper copy and update your CRM.

This sounds so elementary, but it works. And it works well. Being diligent and consistent in your follow up is a powerful tool in building a strong reputation.

## Quote and Dote

If you are providing a price quote, do everything you can to meet with the client and go through it line by line, proving value along the way. Dote on the customer. Do not assume they will contact you. And certainly, do not ignore them once you have sent the quote off assuming your job is done. This happens too often. Opportunities and income generating possibilities are missed. Nicole East, from EastCaan Contracting Ltd., a home renovation company, says:

***"I used to send estimates out to customers and follow up within a few days by email or telephone. My closing rate at the time was 30%. Now, I book a meeting with the customer and go through the quote, line by line to build value and answer any questions or concerns they may have. My closing rate has jumped to 90%!"***

If a meeting is not possible, go through it over the phone. One of my clients, Normandeau Window Coverings, used to simply send the quote out and follow up a few days later. Once they started phoning and going through them line by line, their closing rate also increased.

If you are processing large volumes of quotes and do not have the opportunity to individually attend to each one in person, send an email. Schedule at least three follow up calls:

- Create a reminder for three days later.
- Create a reminder for one month afterwards.
- Create a reminder for three months afterwards.

BADASS SUPERSTARS recognize that there is still much work to do after a quote is delivered. Today people are busy, it is your responsibility as the seller to be proactive in follow up.

**TIPS:**

- **People will rarely be candid and say, "I do not have the money right now."**
- **It is important that you follow up and keep going until you hear the words, "not interested."**

## THE LOST ART OF THANK YOU

**A BADASS knows it is the support of those around him that makes him successful.**

We often forget to say thank you. Always follow up with an email, thanking them for the opportunity, the order, the conversation, etc. Make sure to include specific details. It makes the thank you seem sincere and personal. Tell them that you are looking forward to servicing them further and you are available to help. Writing a thank you card that has genuine appreciation and thought behind it is a lost art that elicits emotion and gratitude.

**TIP: Handwritten thank you cards are best. When done well, with authenticity and genuineness, they evoke an emotional connection.**

With systems in place, you can set aside time to follow up and watch your business, your income, and your promotion possibilities grow. Kieran Longworth, Partner and Sales Expert at the national recruitment firm LOCK SEARCH GROUP says:

***"The most common things salespeople fail to do are the simple things: work hard, listen, do what you say you are going to do, and follow up. As simple as it sounds, it's rare."***

Follow up is the one area that most people neglect to commit to, yet it is the one area that customers have the highest expectations. It is their way to weed out the non-performers and reward the performers with their business and loyalty.

# CHAPTER 12

# *The* NOTEABLES

## DO NOT TALK PRICE

**The BADASS knows that talking price before presenting value will kill the deal.**

Price issues will arise early in all sales conversations. It is the first and the biggest obstacle to overcome. Put off the price conversation for as long as possible. You want to first learn about their situation and gain information on what they are looking for in terms of wants and needs, then you want to make sure you are offering them the right solutions for those needs. Instead, of answering a price inquiry, shift to presenting the features/benefits and create value before discussing price.

***"Almost six in ten buyers want to discuss pricing on the first call."***

—HubSpot

Remember, 94% of sales happen for other reasons. Only 6% of sales are based on price. People naturally resistant and looking for a reason to say NO. Talking price prematurely gives them the excuse they need to walk away, and you will sacrifice the sale. Leave the money conversation until the end. Prove value first.

## TELL STORIES AND GIVE EXAMPLES

Storytelling is the most powerful tool salespeople have to influence, persuade and close the sale.

Stories have huge impact. Tell past customer stories:

- **Negative Stories:** Customer chose competitor product, this is what happened as a result.
- **Positive Stories:** How choosing your product created a positive outcome.
- **Personal Stories:** I use this product, or this is what happened to me.

Negative and personal stories have the most impact because they create validity, believability and evoke emotional connection. A story will be remembered particularly when they can put themselves in, or identify with the situation.

***"Listeners remember stories up to 22 times more often than facts and figures alone."***

—Jerome Bruner

## THE FOUR LANGUAGES OF SELLING

**The BADASS uses knowledge to their advantage.**

To simplify your selling process and achieve faster results, "speak the other person's language" for more efficient and effective communication. Focus on identifying the following Four Personality Profile Types to quickly meet their needs and close more sales. Each is uniquely different with their own priorities and perspectives, but once you know what to look for, you can make more informed, strategic decisions to speed up the sales cycle.

The Four Personality types are:

1. **The Latest and Greatest:** These folks want the biggest, the best, the newest, the brightest, and the most unique. Everything from the newest iPhone to driving a fancy sports car or being identified and associated with the high-end brands that make them feel exclusive. Focus on how your product or service will make them look or feel special, with only the exclusive being able to join the club. They want to stand out and be seen.

**TIP: The Latest and Greatest are quick/emotional decision makers.**

2. **Family and Friends:** This group is all about relationships and loyalty. Tap into how your product or service will improve their relationships and you have won them over… typically for a lifetime as this group is brand loyal and the greatest resource for referrals.

**TIP: The Family and Friend people will need consensus when they purchase, re-affirm they are making the right decision.**

3. **Quality and Value:** People in this group are definitely more cautious in their purchasing decisions. Reinforce how your product or service is of the utmost quality… and then secure the deal by offering them some sort of value-add benefit. These will be the people looking for some sort of discount or special deal; discount, two for one special, promo item for free, etc.

**TIP: The Quality and Value buyers will often be motivated by a beneficial payment method.**

4. **Proof and Documentation:** These are your thinkers. They will need a thorough understanding of the product and/or service to support any purchasing decision. Give them analytics; documentation or data, specification sheets, anything based on facts. They need to support their buying decision with logic.

**TIP: Do not rush to close… they will need time to think about and process their purchasing decision.**

## Presentation Extraordinaire

If you do not have the time or opportunity to ask questions and properly assess your prospects before introducing yourself to them, the best thing you can do is to create a simple strategic presentation that incorporates the benefits that meet the specific buying needs of all four Personality Profile groups.

For example, my daughter is a Sales Rep for a large Canadian Wine Manufacturer. She asked me to help her create a sales strategy for a blowout sales event where she would be standing shoulder to shoulder, beside two dozen competitor representatives. All were tasked with selling a full pallet (56 cases) of their brand as quickly as possible. The goal was to capture the attention of the potential buyers and outsell each other. With potential customers lined up out the door waiting to rush in and quickly scout the product offerings… the strategy was simple; a focused, all-encompassing opening statement to captivate, intrigue and engage. While decking out the location with balloons, signage, and wine glass in brightly coloured giveaway bags to draw the attention of the buyers. She was well prepared with brochures and a rehearsed presentation that went like this:

- "Hi Mr/Mrs Customer… have you seen our FIVE-TIME AWARD WINNING Wine?" (She had specifically chosen this wine as the multiple awards made it unique and special, elevating it to a higher perceived value. These of course would be very appealing to the Latest and Greatest as well as the Quality and Value types).
- She would then hand the customer a specification sheet, verbally confirming the wine's most impressive facts, while mentioning that the document included all the details; history, origin, awards received, composition, characteristic and flavour profile. (Ample research, proof and logic required to support the Proof and Documentation types).
- She would go on to say, "Our 'ABC' wine is a medium bodied, an everyday wine that will appeal to all, perfect for sharing with family and friends." (The vision and lead in required for the Relationship types).
- "It is on sale 'today only' for $ ...that is 40% off the regular price of $$$ …that is a savings of X amount of dollars." (The price breakdown reinforced the savings which was imperative for the Value buyer and the Research type, but it also reinforced urgency, prompting the Latest and Greatest to purchase).

- "And for those who buy in case quantity, you will receive two FREE limited edition, speciality wine glasses as a bonus." (The giveaway was used to bundle the product and assist in moving greater inventory quantities. The gift with purchase was appealing to the Quality and Value types as well as the Latest and Greatest).

In one quick conversation, she presented the product and met the buying needs of all four groups. Using the personality style and purchasing motivators, she sold an entire pallet of wine in less than an hour! Apparently, this was the fastest sell-out the wine store had ever seen in all their years hosting this promotional sale!

## MAKE THEM VIPS

**BADASS SUPERSTARS know how to make everyone in their world feel special.**

Invite them to special events where they can feel special and valued. Hockey Games, Network events, Courses or Training Seminars that you think they would appreciate attending.

At I-XL Building Products Ltd., Pat Adams who was a brilliant marketer and who gave me 100% in allowing me to pursue my creative strategies, chartered a private jet, taking some of our top clients to the manufacturing plant for a private tour detailing the incredible history of the company. That itself was fabulous. But they made it a WOW customer experience by including adding dinner at an exclusive private club and restaurant where everyone could meet and mingle. Before they headed home on the plane, they gave them a gorgeous gift bag filled with quality goodies. To this day, twenty-five years later, people are still talking about those trips.

Pat knew the value of a VIP Experience and made sure to add the little extras, making it a legacy experience. Magnificent!

## STAND OUT AND SURPRISE

**A BADASS SUPERSTAR stands out from the crowd.**

They do the things that surprise their clients, in ways that are unparalleled compared to the other representatives in their field. As a result, they gain respect and become the most memorable.

One of my favorite stories of this was told to me by Malcolm Sissons at I-XL Industries Ltd. He was developing a market for its masonry products in Japan. As can be imagined, language was a significant barrier. A translator was required for all conversations and interactions. Malcolm decided to do more and be more for his clients. He did something which I believe was 'extraordinary'. It spoke volumes about how much he valued his clients. As a busy executive, leading multiple companies, Malcolm took the time to learn some Japanese! He stated,

***"Do the unexpected!<br>They never expected me to speak their language.<br>By taking the extra step,<br>I showed them that I cared."***

Wow! When he told his story, the passion and deep connection he felt for these clients was emanating. He did it from his heart, as a genuine act of kindness for his customer. That is what Superstar Selling is all about.

## ACTION PARALYSIS

**The BADASS SUPERSTAR gets creative in moving buyers off the ledge of indecision.**

When a customer becomes stuck and unable to move out of indecision, there are a few things you can do to help move them forward:

- **Set Minimums:** The grocery chain Superstore does this all the time. "Receive at special price of only $2 when you purchase a minimum of 4."
- **Break Down Costs into Smaller Amounts:** Car dealerships capitalize on this technique. "Only $270 biweekly" breaks the price down from the thousands of dollars required to buy a new car."
- **Remind Them How Easy it is to Get Started:** "Save 10% when you apply today. Only takes minutes to apply." Department stores do this all the time.
- **Create Urgency:** "Act Now" does compel some people to act immediately.
- **Create Scarcity:** "Limited Time Offer" leads people to believe if they don't purchase right away, they will lose out and be unable to receive the offer later.
- **Offer Another Service:** Offer related services to what they have purchased. If they use your lawncare service in summer, ask if they would like to have your snow shovelling service in winter.
- **Now or Never:** This is the last one. 25% discount if you buy today.

# UPSELL TO EXCEL

**Upselling is an opportunity for you to increase your bottom line with minimal effort and little to no risk.**

Your customer already has a need in mind, they trust you, your company and your product, so why not help them by providing the opportunity to offer an additional service, add an additional product, an extended warranty or provide bundles and packages that provide value.

Upselling, just like closing is simply asking a question.

## Do You Want Fries with That?

Have you ever noticed when you go through a line at the fast food restaurant, they will ask, 'Do you want fries with that?" Do the same for your business. When I implemented this sales process at the order desk, asking clients if they needed accessory items, our inside sales division increased by 40%. Almost every sale, thereafter, included an accessory. Not only did it increase sales, but also served the client reducing the annoying second trip they would have to make as a result of forgetting to pick up those 'extra little items.'

## Disservice Not to Offer Another Service

Providing an opportunity to purchase 'related services or items' only makes sense. If you are providing lawn care services, why wouldn't you offer to provide aeration services or sprinkler blowouts for them? Make sure that when you offer additional services, that they are related to the original need. By not offering your services, you are opening the door for your competition.

## Bundles Provide Benefits

Cable, fast food and appliance companies are great at this. You can buy your internet, cable and phone separately, or you can buy a 'bundle' and 'save a bit of money'. Purchase a kids' meal and get the 'free' toy. Add an extended warranty 'for only a few dollars more'. Regardless of which method you use, upselling is part of our society. What can you do with your products and services to upsell and add to your bottom line?

## CREATE NEXT APPOINTMENT

The best time to close a deal is now. If the prospect leaves, chances are you will have lost the sale because purchasing is based on emotion. Yes, the longer people discuss or negotiate, the more they will want to close the deal but if they walk away, chances are they won't come back.

We also know that today's customer and the purchasing process takes multiple visits. It is for that reason that one should always book the next appointment before the conversation ends. Just like the buyer who walks away is less likely to come back and make the purchase, if you leave without booking another appointment, your opportunity to do so after the fact substantially deteriorates.

## ASK FOR REFERRAL

**The BADASS loves introductions to new people.**

At the end of every introduction you make, conversation you have, client you talk to, ask them for a referral. Too often, people introduce themselves or conduct business and assume that others will automatically pass on their name as a referral. It doesn't happen. You must ask the question, "Do you know anyone who might be looking for (product or service)?" so that it transfers from the right (creative) side of the brain to the left (logic) side. When people stop to think about it, it transfers into their memory. When the topic comes up at a later point in time, they will remember to mention you as a result of you asking the questions versus you simply making a statement.

**TIP: Ninety-two per cent of buyers trust referrals from people they know. And, 9 out of 10 buying decisions are made with peer recommendations.**

***"Asking for the referral is a habit we should all get into. Forty-seven per cent of top performers ask for referrals consistently, versus only 26% of non-top performers."***

—HubSpot

***"Salespeople who actively seek out and exploit referrals earn four to five times more than those who don't."***

—Brevet

Referral-based selling is the secret to selling success in selling today, as the customer automatically transfers trust. Asking for the referral at the end of every call or conversation is an opportunity to maximize your credibility and income.

## POOR PRESENTATIONS LINGER LONG AFTER

**The BADASS knows what is at stake today is much different than yesterday.**

Unfortunately, we do not ace all our selling presentations. When you do a poor presentation or something goes wrong that you cannot control, remember selling has changed. You must take action to resolve.

We live in a new, very visible world where our poor performance can have significant consequences. Social media reviews, social proof and word of mouth have made the stakes are higher today than ever before:

- People tell five times to twenty-five as many people about bad service they have received versus good service.
- Only 4% of dissatisfied customers let the company know. Ninety-one per cent of the 95% of business will never return.
- It takes twelve positive experiences to make up for one unresolved negative experience.

Improving our skillset, being prepared and practicing has never been so important.

## THE NOT-SO-FUN SIDE OF SELLING

**A BADASS handles bad news with character and grace.**

As salespeople, we often get bad news we know our customer is not going to be happy about. A late production date, the product was discontinued, you cannot fulfil the promise made… whatever it is, regardless of how it is, ALWAYS be totally honest.

As Jeff Kelly, a highly regarded Customer Service Representative and one of my past clients stated:

> ***"Salespeople just cannot be straight up and tell it exactly as it is. They need to tell the truth regardless of how bad the news is, or how it makes your company look."***

Too often salespeople avoid delivering the bad news hoping that under some miraculous circumstance it will simply go away, and the customer will never have to find out. Big mistake.

## THE COOKIE JAR

**The BADASS knows character outshines charisma.**

I liken it to a cookie jar. Each time we do something to earn trust, create value for, or serve our customer well, we get to put an imaginary cookie in the cookie jar. Each time we mess up, a cookie gets eaten. How badly we mess up determines how many cookies are munched away. As we build and strengthen our relationships with our customers, we add more cookies. The goal is to make sure your jar is always overflowing because there will be moments when, like it or not, it can be wiped out. And in those moments, you can never go wrong doing the right thing.

- **Tell Your Customer Right Away:** If you have bad news, and we always do, muster up the courage and tell your customer right away, giving them the time to make alternate arrangements. Yes, it might result in you losing the sale, but in the long term, you will gain something more valuable—trust, respect and a stronger relationship.

- **Give Your Customer All the Facts:** Do not hold back information. Give them all the facts and be completely honest. Do not lead your customer to believe a better outcome will happen, if you know it never will. Allow them the opportunity to do what is right for them. Remember serve versus self-serve.

- **Do not Omit, Misrepresent or Lie:** They all fall under the category of dishonest.

- **Work Hard to Find Resolution:** Deliver the bad news with a few alternatives or resolutions in hand. Assure your customer you are going to do everything possible to find a solution.

**TIP: People know that errors are going to happen. It is about how quickly and professionally you can resolve it that matters.**

- **Keep in Touch:** Even if you have nothing to offer, follow up regularly to let your client know what you are doing and what the status of the situation is.

As Malcolm Sissons from I-XL adamantly believes,

***"A problem is an opportunity in disguise. Face the music, step up, and take the wrath. Customers remember your mistakes forever! Do not duck out, hoping it will go away."***

Non-communication of any type is a killer! Your customer deserves to be informed at all times. Success in selling is based on the strength of your relationships. The world is full of salespeople who lack integrity and fail to do the right thing out of fear—do not be one of those people. Be accountable, step up and take responsibility. In today's selling, if you want to overcome the skepticism and resistance that exists today, we must maintain our BADASS mindset, attitude and skillset.

# CHAPTER 13

# *Final* THOUGHTS

**The BADASS Understands Success is a Journey.**

***"Success is no accident. It is hard work, perseverance, learning, studying, sacrifice and most of all, love of what you are doing or learning to do."***

—Pele

I have trained many people who, like me, have gone from adequate to outstanding by implementing small but effective changes. They have climbed the ladder to career success and are now earning incomes they only dreamed of before adopting the these seemingly basic concepts.

An incremental learning strategy is the secret to success. Achieving small wins and tackling challenges one step at a time builds confidence and fuels the courage required to tackle the next step.

Selling today is all about differentiating yourself, your product and your company from the pack and creating impact. Regardless of how it is achieved, selling must be based on the unique advantages we bring to the market in order to veer away from price and commodity comparison.

Whether you are a seasoned veteran wanting to upgrade your skillset to a modern approach, mid-way in your career looking for advancement, or just starting out, implementing these simple, yet reliable sales tips, techniques, approaches and strategies makes building rapport, overcoming objections and closing easy.

It is doing the small things that allow BADASS SUPERSTARS to stand out amongst their peers. They are the go-to representatives because people trust they will always follow through on their promises and commitments, and know the priority is to be a partner in helping to support and create success for the client. Honest, transparent and accountable, they debunk all the old stereotypes focusing instead on building trust-based, customer-centric relationships. They think outside the box, continually looking for ways to create value and simplicity. They delve deeper, sell better and achieve faster results. They are BADASS SUPERSTARS. They are truly in a category of their own making.

***"If I can do it, and the people I have trained can do it, you too can become a BADASS SUPERSTAR!"***

—Jackie Rainforth

They will win the race, if only by a nose, catapulting their sales, careers and businesses skywards to new heights.

Wishing you unbridled success on your journey!

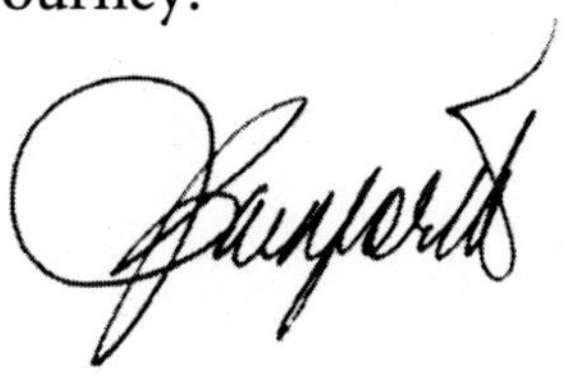

Jackie Rainforth
info@rainmakersgroup.ca

*Wherever you are in the world, there is nothing preventing your from achieving BADASS SUPERSTAR STATUS. If you are interested in having me speak at your next event, receive my blogs, vlogs or newsletters, email me using info@ rainmakersgroup.ca. Say you heard about becoming a BADASS in my book and you'll receive a special bonus of a FREE 30-minute sales strategy session! My gift to you.*

*Can't wait to hear from you!*

# ABOUT THE AUTHOR

JACKIE RAINFORTH is a record-breaking, award-winning sales expert, professional speaker, learning and development facilitator and author. Nicknamed the RAINMAKER by her peers, she has a 25-year track record of top sales performance in corporate sales, sales management and executive sales leadership. As the entrepreneurial founder and owner of a highly successful sales agency she received the highly coveted RBC Canadian Women Entrepreneur of Canada Award. She is a BADASS SUPERSTAR. After surviving a near-death scuba diving incident that changed her life, it has become her mission to share her secrets to success so you too can become a BADASS SUPERSTAR.

# REFERENCES

*The Career Planner*, Jean Twenge PhD., author of *iGen, Why Today's Super Connected Kids are Growing Up Less Rebellious, More Tolerant, Less Happy.*

ca.finance.yahoo.com/news/boomers-vs-millennials-look-financial-201000886.html

www.goodreads.com/book/show/33268384-igen

LEADERSHIP IQ/INC Magazine/FORBES Magazine/College Field 2014/Global Human

Capital Trends/Deloitte/Glassdoor Data Labs/Statista International

Dudovskiy, Joh (2013) Business Research *"The Evolution of Selling"*.

Forbes.com/sites/davidsturt2018/03/08/20-shocking-workplace-stats-you-need-to-know

www.Stevepatrizi.com/2012/10/23/the-new-marketing-sales-funnel

Forbes-com.cdn 2107/12/31 Prof David DeSteno

Leblanc, Mark (2003), *Grow Your Business*!, Andover MN, Expert Publishing Inc.

www.newvoicemedia.com/resources/the-real-cost-of -poor-prospecting

www.superoffice.com/blog/6-sales-prospecting-tips-for-todays-sales-professional

Rosen, Keith (2008) *"Coaching Sales People Into Sales Champions Hoboken"*, New Jersey, John Wiley & Sons Inc.

hbr.org/2018/10/how-to-blow-a-presentation-to-the-c-suite

www.newvoicemedia.com/blog/10-trends-changing-customer-expectations

prewswire.com/Yeslifecycle-Marketing-july/10/2017

Shore, Jeff (2008) *"New Homes Sales"*, Gaithersburg, MD, Signature Book Printer.

www.huffingtonpost.ca/Workaholic/12/06/2017

www.forbes.com/Millennials-Earn-20%-less/01/14/2017

Tracy, Brian (The Psychology of Selling) CD Series.

www.inc.com/4 *"Ways Your Emotions Can Screw Up Your Decisions"*

www.blog.hubspot.com/30-Inspirational-Quotes-From-*"How-to-Win-Friends-and-Influence-People"*/DavidLyKhim

www.radicati.com/wp/wp-content/uploads/2015/02/Email-Statistics-Report-2015-2019-Executive-Summary.pdf www.smallbusiness.chron.com/The-Advantages-of-a-Product-Differentiation-Strategy/06/29/18

www.hingemarketing.com/Differentiation-Strategy-for-the-Professional-Services-Firm/02/14/18

SmartInsights.com/Drive-your-sales-with-7-powerful-emotions/02/10/15

www.ScienceDaily.com/The psychology-of-gift-giving-and-receiving/12/22/2014

b2bmarketing.net/5-Steps-to-Understanding-Your-customer's-buying-process/05/18/16

Selling Power e-distribution@sellingpowermx.com/Choices

www.guided-selling.org/gender-selling

www.blog.hubspot.com/How-to-be-Persistent-In-Sales-Without-Being-Annoying-Your-Prospects/NitiShah

www.Forbes.com/Neuroscience-Explains-Why-You-Need-To-Write-Down-Your-Goals/04/15/18

www.adaptiveneuroscience.com/2015/10/12/neuroscience-of-selling

www.hubspot.com/sales/sales-statisticsAjaFrost

www.dreamgrow/21-Social-Media-Marketing-Statistic-You-Need-to-Know-in-2018/05/05/2018

www.theheadhunters.ca;/generational gap series: Baby Boomers in the workplace-Cards/02/27/2018

www.leadresponsemanagement.org/lrm_study

www.Elle.com/Are-Women-More-Likely-to-Use-Just-Gschwandtner, Gerhard (2007) The Ultimate Sales Training Workshop, New York NY, McGraw Hill.

www.square2marketing.com/blog/will-artificial-intelligence-cause-sales-roles-to-disappear

Behrens, Bill (2015) Let Your True Colors Shine, True Colors International.

www.smallbiztrends.com/2018/07/real-time-response-to-customers.html

www.forbes.com/sites/ryanerskine/2017/09/19/20-online-reputation-statistics-that-every-business-owner-needs-to-know/#5cf9e2b4cc5c

Bruner, Jerome (1985) Actual Minds, Possible Worlds - The Jerusal*em-Harvard Lectures* Harvard University Press.